Standards-Based Lessons for Tech-Savvy Students:

A Multiple Intelligences Approach

By Walter McKenzie

Your Trusted Library-to-Classroom Connection.
Books, Magazines, and Online

This book is dedicated to my wife Carleen and my children Christopher and Mallory, without whose support and love I could not have completed this effort.

Library of Congress Cataloging-in-Publication Data

McKenzie, Walter.
  Standards-based lessons for tech-savvy students : a multiple intelligence
approach / by Walter McKenzie.
       p. cm.
  Includes bibliographical references and index.
  ISBN 1-58683-125-9 (paperback)
  1. Education--Effect of technological innovations on--United States. 2.
Educational technology--United States. 3. Information technology--United
States. I. Title.
LB1028.3.M397 2004
371.33--dc22

                              2003026304

Publishing by Linworth Publishing, Inc.
480 East Wilson Bridge Road, Suite L
Worthington, OH 43085

ISBN: 1-58683-125-9

5 4 3 2 1

Table of Contents _____

Table of Figures

About the Author

Walter McKenzie is an educator and lifelong learner who has been integrating technology and multiple intelligences theory into instruction over the past two decades. He resides with his wife Carleen and his children Christopher and Mallory in Massachusetts, where he serves as Director of Information Systems for the Salem Public Schools. His first book published in 2002 is entitled *Multiple Intelligences and Instructional Technology: A Manual for Every Mind* (ISTE).

Walter writes and teaches for Connected University, where he has served as Chair for the Departments of Instruction, Reading & Language Arts, and Technology Integration for K–12. Walter also hosts an education Web site entitled "The One and Only Surfaquarium" <http://surfaqaurium.com> and his "Innovative Teaching" weekly newsletter, which currently boasts more than 2,800 subscribers.

Introduction

The Information Age is upon us and with it comes new demands on educators. Today's students will work in a world where information is the coin of the realm and those who know how to work with it effectively will be the most successful. They will have to collaborate, think flexibly, create solutions to existing problems, and create new ways of delivering information to consumers. The classroom will need to reflect these demands so that students can develop these skills through practical, meaningful experiences. How can educators find the time and resources to meet these new demands?

Standards-Based Lessons for Tech-Savvy Students: A Multiple Intelligences Approach offers a unit model that is built to accommodate and integrate our evolving understanding about learning at the dawn of the Information Age. Allowing for all of the different student orientations to learning, *Standards-Based Lessons for Tech-Savvy Students: A Multiple Intelligences Approach* empowers teachers by integrating state and national standards through a wealth of rich, real world, authentic tasks. Technology provides opportunities to extend these learning experiences across all the domains of learning within the classroom and to worlds beyond the traditional scope of the classroom. The result is a myriad of opportunities for wonder moments—those incredible learning experiences we keep with us for a lifetime.

Herein you will find not only a working model for instruction, but a conceptual framework that addresses all of the needs of the Information Age classroom. Within this framework, seven units are presented that offer the context for engaging, motivating, and rewarding learning in the classroom. It is my sincere hope that these examples will serve as a springboard for your own new unit development—units that will build bridges for students regardless of their orientation to learning.

Chapter 1

Moments of Wonder

Reform from the Bottom Up

Over the past 30 years, public education has been rife with reform. These movements have identified and targeted important issues in education: early childhood math concept development, holistic approaches to language instruction, curriculum mapping and integration, assessment of student progress, and effective schools, to name a few. And while each of these reform movements has had its own unique charisma, the movements have at the same time all been striving to reach the same lofty goal: effective instruction and improved student learning. While the orientation often changes, the end is always the same: to effectively promote learning in meaningful, long lasting ways. Well-intended initiatives often attempt to influence the dialogue on educational reform by advocating specific approaches to instruction. Educators dutifully implement these programs in the best interests of children, yet the staying power of such initiatives relies in the commitment of educators to stay the course. Any program that is given less than five years to succeed is, for all intents and purposes, dead on arrival. Schools are institutions, and institutions need time to absorb new ideas.

Grassroots reform movements tend to have more staying power, largely because there is ownership on the part of educators for the initiative's success. They have been tested in the trenches and gain credibility through word of mouth, group sharing, conference presentations, discussion lists, and publications until they eventually are absorbed into the mainstream of educational practice. Once absorbed, the reform becomes assimilated into a format that is acceptable across the spectrum of educational pedagogies. It may not look the same as it did at its inception, but its impact on the ways we think about, discuss, and implement instruction is significant.

What characterizes an idea ripe for grassroots support? Any idea that puts the best interests of students first is a good candidate. Innovative approaches to instruction that help teachers reach students in new and different ways are also likely to get noticed. Consider the popularity of multiple intelligences theory. For decades, teachers have been utilizing strategies to reach students who were not necessarily part of contemporary trends in instruction. Howard Gardner appears with a new way to look at human intelligence and many educators take notice. Why? Teachers have become more reflective practitioners. They have examined the way they were taught and the ways they in turn teach their students. Gardner helps educators explain why everyone doesn't learn in the same manner. Multiple intelligence theory also prompts educators to think differently about learners. As society changes, we work to meet each child's needs on a more individualized basis. Verbal and logical tasks no longer seem appropriate for the entire school day. Children need authentic, hands-on, real-life experiences to develop ideas conceptually before they can transform their understandings symbolically on paper. This grassroots movement is especially striking against the backdrop of standards and testing. To the casual observer, it may seem that there is a juxtaposition of multiple intelligences theory and standards and testing. On closer examination, though, we realize that both of these trends in education are necessary to sustain one another. Meeting the different paths to learning is essential for demonstrating learning on standardized tests.

Expanding Understanding

Consider the many different modalities students use to learn. There was a time when three learning styles were enough to explain the different paths to learning. Students were either visual, auditory, or kinesthetic, and once a child was labeled appropriately the teacher could theoretically teach him or her through that specific learning style all day across all subject areas. If you were a visual learner in math, then you were surely a visual learner in reading, science, and social studies. Once labeled, always labeled. Yet teachers could see in their students many different paths to learning aside from the eyes, ears, and hands. What about those students who were very social and always seemed to influence the class through discussion? Or those students who excelled in music and the fine and performing arts? Or those who seemed so incredibly linear and logical they had difficulty any time the classroom routine changed?

Teachers haven't been sure what to call it, but they have known there are more than three ways children learn in their classrooms. Instinctively, they provide a wide range of learning experiences, hoping to catch as many children as possible in a net of learning. Still, when administrators come to observe, it isn't easy trying to justify a room ebbing and flowing in a tide of varied activity. The ideal has been one current of class activity, flowing in the same direction toward the mastery of a single objective. Time on task, structured lessons, and formal assessments have been the hallmarks of effective instruction for decades.

Then in the 1980s came brain research, which offered evidence that the human mind actually made use of many different paths to understanding. For teachers, this explained what they had been seeing in students for a long time, and it gave credence to many of the things teachers were already doing in the classroom to meet the needs of learners. As teachers learned more, they took to this new knowledge like fish to water. The rising tide of change this has created has lifted all of us with it. There is no turning back!

The Age of Standardization

Today the trend for state and even national standardized testing across all grade levels seems to impose new conditions on how we teach. Educators are under tremendous pressure to have students pass these tests in order to document student learning, thereby documenting effective teaching. For many well-meaning educators, this has meant a return to "drill and skill" practices to promote the mastery of basic facts and understandings for which these standardized tests typically test. "If I have to get them ready for these tests," one teacher reasoned, "I don't have time to be teaching the way I like to. They have to learn using pencil and paper because that's how they will be tested." In the learning styles model, this would be very true. Students need to learn to excel in pencil and paper tasks because that will best prepare them for required standardized testing.

But think about this assumption for a moment: is it true that if you learn new material through one learning modality, you can only demonstrate your understanding of that material through the same avenue? If you learn to fish by fishing while sitting on a riverbank, can you only share your knowledge of the experience by returning to the river to show your expertise? If you learn about ancient Egypt by reading, are you then unable to create a diorama model of the Valley of the Kings? If you learn about our solar system through lecture, are you then incapable of sharing your knowledge of the planets via PowerPoint? Of course not. The very definition of learning mastery is to be able to apply a learned fact, skill, or concept in a new and unfamiliar context.

The old learning styles model served education well in its time, but we need to question the assumptions we still hold about internalizing new ideas and recalling new ideas to demonstrate learning. Children do not have to learn using pencil and paper in order to be successful on standardized tests. Certainly it is appropriate to have students practice standardized test formats to help them prepare for testing, but that is much different from teaching to a verbal modality because the tests are verbal in nature.

In fact, quite to the contrary, if learning is experiential in nature, then forcing children to learn through pencil and paper tasks actually limits their ability to learn as much as they can before standardized testing takes place. Could a teacher actually be handicapping a student with a strong kinesthetic, musical, interpersonal profile by subjecting him or her to months of pencil and paper instruction? Could that same student be much more successful in identifying correct answers on a standardized test if he or she were able to master the curriculum through all the paths to learning?

Question your assumptions and see what you decide. Yes it is frightening to let go of preconceived notions, taking the risk of empowering students to master their own learning, but it is the only way to provide for those moments of wonder when students truly understand. These "wonder moments" transcend any given school year or curriculum. They are moments of understanding that stay with us for a lifetime. They are meaningful, poignant moments in our educational career that still make us come alive when we recall them today. Is there any doubt that students who experience wonder moments as they learn do well on standardized tests?

Moments of Wonder

So what do wonder moments look like? Consider other educators' responses when asked to identify a moment of wonder they can recall when they truly learned something in a remarkable way:

> I would have to say one of the most memorable moments of my education came when I was in the third grade. I remember vividly that as we were learning our handwriting, my teacher, Mrs. Schwartz (loved her), took us outside to practice our letters by writing them in the moist sandbox. This teacher as an entity resonates in my memory. I can probably think of 10–20 clear memories (specific things she said in certain circumstances even) from this teacher from the third grade. I remember thinking that it was amazing that I could take something so concrete such as how to write the cursive alphabet and have fun doing that in the sandbox. Before then, it was as if the two concepts could not be related.
>
> *Niki Kigerl*
> *Aurora, Colorado*

> My "wow" moment actually came as a I was fifth-grade teacher. As I was teaching a geometry lesson, I ran across a visual explanation of how a triangle measures 180 degrees. Before that moment, I never had a clue how to explain it or how "they" figured out that a shape with straight lines and angles could be related to a circle. As I realized how simple it really was, the kids got as excited as I did.
>
> The moment that I realized the relationship and how it could be demonstrated in a hands-on activity, my mind hyperspaced to how I could relate this to other math objectives that I had been trying (unsuccessfully) to show the students.
>
> *Linda Villarreal*
> *San Antonio, Texas*

> Mrs. Strelich was my fifth-grade teacher. Imagine that she was just like the *Magic School Bus* teacher—the children's book, Mrs. Foozlesomething. During our studies of the California Gold Rush, she would bring equipment that was used to pan for gold. We would go outside in the playground and actually pan for gold (little rocks that she painted gold). During the week, we would earn gold for assignments completed. Everyone worked so hard to earn gold. It was the most fun time I have ever had at school. We wrote reports, colored maps, panned for gold and then—when we had learned all we could learn about the gold rush days—all the parents would bake huge amounts of food and we would have a huge party. The students would have to purchase their food with gold. The better you did throughout the lessons, the more gold you had to spend on delicious food. It was spectacular! I will never forget it.
>
> *Kristi McCreedy*
> *Bakersfield, California*

When I was in 11th grade, in World History Class, I had to do a report on Queen Isabella and King Ferdinand. Along with our 10-page report, we were required to submit a project. The only rule for this project was that it had to teach the class about our report subject without us actually using the written report. At the time, I thought that this was the hardest assignment I had ever had. It was so much easier to put together a poster or booklet, when given all the instructions to do so. But ... this time I was on my own! I had nothing for a while; then just a few days before everything was due, I came up with it. I would make puppets and then perform for the class. I worked on those puppets for hours after school and sewed King and Queen hand puppets. I asked a friend to help with the "show" and wrote a script for us depicting the time during which they were involved with Christopher Columbus. It might not seem too profound to anyone else, but I had to dig deep within and find a part of myself. I found a way I liked to teach.

Danielle Simard
Nashua, New Hampshire

As a child, I was always interested in rock collecting. I would go into the big field next to our neighborhood and pick up beautiful and interesting rocks for my personal collection. Imagine my delight when I found out that the project required in eighth-grade science was to accumulate a collection of rocks! I was in heaven. Up to this point, I just collected rocks that were good looking or interesting. This project required me to go beyond the rocks "good looks." I got to (got to, not had to) find out about the different types of rocks (e.g., igneous, sedimentary), their properties, chemical composition, how they were made, and so on. This project opened doors of knowledge and wonder that I hadn't yet experienced. My parents found a cigar box for me to display them in. I had never experienced such motivation on a school project before. I was very proud of my project. That pride sustained me for a long time.

Tim Wehrle
Machesney Park, Illinois

I attended Millsaps College in Jackson, Mississippi. As a freshman, I took an interdisciplinary course in humanities called "Heritage." A lot of the freshman thought we were crazy to be signed up for a class that met five days a week and twice on Tuesdays and Thursdays, but those of us in it loved it. Dr. Sallis led our group discussions on Friday mornings and connected the dots for me. We took a period of time in history and studied more than just what was happening in Western civilization. We studied all of the art, philosophy, religion, and music for that period of time. We had guest lecturers from every conceivable specialty. It was the most important class I ever took. My fires for learning were finally lit.

Lisa Reese
St. Francisville, Louisiana

My most rewarding learning experience dates back to the fall of 1989. Growing up in post-war Germany, the Berlin Wall was as much a part of the German history as Beethoven, Wagner, or Goethe. That fall, sitting in my dorm room, watching the evening news, I saw the future of German history being written. I watched my fellow countrymen defiant and without fear walking on top of the Berlin Wall, using sledgehammers to break pieces out of it to reunite the people of a country divided by political ideologies.

Having a certain distance to a situation, looking from the outside in, rather than from the inside out, opens different perspectives, necessary for a balanced judgment. This learning did not take place in a formal classroom, but it taught me an important lesson.

I had started my studies in journalism, only a month before the fall of the Berlin Wall. Comparing the U.S. news reporting to the reports I was receiving from my parents and friends in Wiesbaden, I discovered how the cultural background of the reporter influenced a viewpoint.

Detaching oneself from a situation and the emotions involved allows one to make a more balanced, higher quality judgment. In working with international students, that has been incredibly helpful. While it may sound simple, this learning experience had a major impact on my life. My international education has taught me to make a decision only after considering diverse cultures, traditions, and values and how they influence different viewpoints.

Udo Fluck
Missoula, Montana

Learning Contexts

For each of these educators, the moment they describe is a life-altering event in their growth as a person. The content itself is inextricably linked to the emotions and recollections that provide the context for the learning. While the mastered content can still be recalled, it is done so as part of the larger human experience that takes place when a wonder moment occurs. Can every lesson be a wonder moment? No, it isn't humanly possible to have all the senses function at that level of heightened stimulation all the time. Then how do these accounts help us in improving instruction? By keeping them in mind when developing instruction that is full of rich, hands-on, real-world experiences, educators allow students to apply skills and concepts in meaningful ways. In this way, all children can experience moments of wonder.

Note the common denominator in each moment of wonder shared. The opportunity for people to fully learn and express themselves using their strengths and their orientation to learning is the key. We can't design moments of wonder for children, because learning is a uniquely personal experience. But by designing units that incorporate everything we now know about how children learn, we can maximize the possibilities for those wonder moments each and every day in our classrooms.

In this book you will learn to design and implement units that emphasize important concepts, ask higher-level questions, incorporate instructional technologies, accommodate all the different paths to learning, and measure student understanding in meaningful, authentic ways.

Building Understanding:

1. Identify a moment of wonder in your own educational career. How is it similar to the experiences shared in this chapter? What seem to be the common elements of wonder moments?

2. Do you hold to the conviction that in order for students to perform well on standardized tests they must be taught using pencil and paper tasks? Why or why not? Give an example from your own experience.

3. Is it surprising that breakthroughs in brain research seem to coincide with the proliferation of instructional technology? Why or why not?

Chapter | 2 |

Technology as an

Integration Tool

A Tool for Instruction

Ask any veteran of the classroom and you'll hear tales of trends and initiatives from the past. They've seen the bandwagons come and go. And the longer they have stayed in the profession, the more convinced they are that there is nothing new under the sun! Consider technology: calculators, overhead projectors, tape recorders, televisions, VCRs, and computers. As more technology arrives in the classroom, expectations grow for its impact on instruction. Early on the assumption was that the presence of technology in the classroom in and of itself would create changes in how teachers teach and children learn. An interesting phenomenon began to occur, however. In any given faculty, certain teachers would embrace a technology and make use of it in instruction, but in general the technology would not take hold school-wide. A teacher who embraced technology was set apart in the minds of staff members and typically became known as the "technology guru" of the building.

In an effort to take advantage of these technology-users, administrators have instituted programs that encourage (and in some cases even require) technology training for staff and technology integration into instruction. These well-intended initiatives have made inroads in schools because they set an expectation whereby all teachers were to be using technology in instruction in some way, shape, or form. While this has been measured in terms of seat time using technology, the quality of technology integration has been an elusive goal that educators have had a much harder time defining, let alone measuring. The emerging baseline consists of teachers making use of technology as much as they are required to do so, with occasional high-end technology users found on any given faculty. Administrators in turn have identified this baseline and use it to measure technology use in terms of seat hours. High-end users are recognized and rewarded by receiving more access to technology dollars and technology seat time, as less interested colleagues forfeit their seats at the table. And the cycle perpetuates itself.

The school library media specialist can be an active advocate for effective integration of technology across the curriculum, supporting teachers when they are ready to learn. The library media specialist is in a unique position to see the big picture of the school program, with knowledge of instructional media that allows him or her to suggest all kinds of electronic and traditional resources to enrich instruction. Coupled with a working knowledge of technology integration, the library media specialist can be a powerful agent for change.

Levels of Technology Integration

Dr. Chris Moersch has developed a system for measuring the quality of technology use in instruction, known as LoTi (Levels of Technology integration). Based on his work with teachers around the country, Moersch developed this system of identifying levels of technology integration to prompt a dialogue among educators on its nature and characteristics. In the LoTi model, there are six levels of integration, ranging from non-use to expansion and refinement. The levels are not necessarily hierarchical. Each level is legitimate in its own right, depending on the instructional task at hand. In some cases, non-use of technology is very appropriate. Likewise, in some instances, use of technology at the infusion or integration level may be highly inappropriate. The instructional objective dictates the appropriate level of technology to be utilized. Let's take a closer look at each of LoTi's six levels.

Non-Use does not imply the complete lack of use of all technologies, but specifically the lack of digital technologies. Traditional instructional technologies such as lecture, textbooks, workbooks, and overhead projectors may be observed. The point is that not using technology in a lesson is an option, and that an effective traditional lesson is preferable to a lesson that uses technology ineffectively. Effective use of technology in instruction can be defined as seamless, transparent use of technology in achieving an instructional goal. It is incidental in reaching the instructional goal and is not forced into the lesson or contrived as an unnecessary extra step in the learning process. Ineffective use of technology usually occurs when it is included simply for its own sake: using a word processor to type out vocabulary sentences, graphing software when manipulative materials help develop the concept more successfully, or a slideshow application when a final work project may be better presented as a hands-on demonstration. The Non-use category for technology integration allows for traditional lessons that do not need to force use of technology in order to be successful.

Awareness is a technology-centered level in which the intended instruction is actually controlled by the technology. While the teacher makes use of technology in a lesson, it is not part of the overall instructional program. For the most part, technology literacy is the goal: keyboarding, navigation, and Web-based researching are all good examples. The emphasis is on technology skills rather than academic content, and technology access is offered only at a set time during the lesson. Again, there is nothing wrong with the Awareness level of technology use; it should not be frowned upon as a less-desirable level than any of the others in the LoTi model. There is a need for this level of lesson in instruction. Consider Ms. Santana, who is beginning a month-long Economics WebQuest with her class. Before she can delve into the meat of the project, she wisely plans lessons on the structure of a WebQuest, information literacy skills, and the proper procedures for saving and citing Internet resources. Each of these lessons will be developed at the awareness level, and each will promote student success when students actually begin their work in the WebQuest she has planned. By mindfully including Awareness level lessons in preparation for the higher-level tasks that lie ahead, Ms. Santana demonstrates sound principles of lesson planning and instructional design.

Exploration is a teacher-centered, teacher-directed level in which technology is used to master content at the lower levels of Bloom's Taxonomy. The primary purpose of technology use at this point is to increase student interest and time on task. Often technology integration at the Exploration level is an extension or enrichment of learning that has already taken place. This can be a precarious use of technology, because it runs the risk of a cookie-cutter approach in which all students are expected to create the same product using an assigned application. More than any other level of LoTi, Exploration is where teachers also run the risk of forcing technology use in some contrived way in instruction. Having said this, the Exploration level can be extremely useful for reinforcement of concepts, guided practice of skills, and simulations that require students to apply their learning in a new and different context. Because the teacher selects student learning experiences with technology, these lessons tend to be more finite in opportunities for higher-order thinking skills, creativity, and critical analysis. Exploration level lessons are an important part of an overall technology program, but they should not be the main form of technology integration used in instruction.

Infusion is a second teacher-centered level of integration, making more authentic use of technology tools in achieving instructional goals. At this level, productivity tools, content software, and Internet resources are utilized to modify lessons that were taught using traditional media in the past. The emphasis remains on the instructional objective, and the technology used is not the only means for achieving the learning goal. A good example of this is the popular M&M graphing lesson in which students open a bag of the candies, sort them by color, use the candies to create a picture graph of the distribution of colors found in the bag, and then transfer the data from the picture graph into a spreadsheet application to make the transition from traditional to digital representation. The learning that takes place is highly motivated, memorable, and easily applied across disciplines, as students have additional opportunities to analyze data and represent their findings in a spreadsheet. At the Infusion level, technology is used with few management problems because there is little variation in the ways it is used for instruction. The true advantage of the Infusion level lesson is that it allows the teacher to provide adaptations in activities, assessments, and materials for students with strengths in different paths to learning.

Integration is a student-centered level of technology integration in which students engage in higher-order thinking activities through inquiry, problem solving, and product making in response to a specific task. The digital tools used at this level go beyond straightforward productivity (writing, publishing, data analysis) to more sophisticated applications such as semantic mapping, video editing and production, and multimedia presentations. These tools are fully integrated into the learning task and help students to demonstrate higher levels of understanding in their work. In short, an Integration level lesson would not be able to be accomplished without the presence of technology. Students have and make choices throughout the lesson, and they collaborate with one another to complete the assignment as they plan, implement, and evaluate their answer to the question at hand. The technology also impacts assessment choices students can make as they opt to communicate knowledge, analyze data, synthesize ideas, and evaluate work products. The Integration level is open-ended in the ways students can match technology to their learning strengths to successfully master skills and concepts identified by the teacher.

Expansion and Refinement is also student-centered and completely constructivist in its approach to instruction. At this level, the teacher does not identify an instructional objective for the class. Students select and use technology to investigate topics, to create original products, to communicate knowledge, and to demonstrate mastery of complex skills and concepts. Technology is used by students for authentic problem-solving tasks based in real-world experiences throughout a unit of study. Most significantly, students have access to (and an understanding of) all kinds of technology tools. As a unit of study is implemented, students seek ways to integrate new uses of technology into their learning and develop new skills as they need them. While there is no hierarchy in the LoTi model, the Expansion and Refinement level is certainly one that can only be achieved over time, as the teacher becomes comfortable enough with technology to allow students full access to its potential in the classroom. This level is also the most optimal for addressing each of the paths to learning, which we know exist in every child. If the teacher allows student choice, then technology will provide the tools that empower students to make those choices successful.

The key to the LoTi model is to keep in mind that all these levels of integration are important. Because each is well-defined with distinct, observable characteristics, LoTi is a great way to observe technology use in a classroom, a computer lab, or across an entire building and determine the quality of technology integration taking place. Having teachers make use of technology in instruction is a start, having them use technology effectively to accommodate the learning needs of all your students is the goal.

A Technology Integration Checklist

With the LoTi model in mind, consider the level at which you typically integrate technology into instruction. Use the checklist below to help you reflect on your technology integration practices:

Non-use

_____ Traditional technology
_____ Technology is not necessary to successfully implement lessons
_____ Lower levels of Blooms Taxonomy
_____ Verbal and logical paths to learning emphasized
_____ Typically one—no more than any two—paths to learning addressed

Awareness

_____ Technology-centered lessons
_____ Focuses on technology skills and literacy
_____ Lower levels of Bloom's Taxonomy
_____ Verbal and logical paths to learning emphasized
_____ Typically one—no more than any two—paths to learning addressed

Exploration

_____ Teacher-centered lessons
_____ Technology used to extend or enrich learning that has taken place
_____ Cookie-cutter approach to technology
_____ Lower levels of Bloom's Taxonomy
_____ Up to three paths to learning addressed

Infusion

_____ Teacher-centered lessons
_____ Makes use of digital productivity tools
_____ Little variation in the ways technology is used for instruction
_____ Mid levels of Bloom's Taxonomy
_____ Up to three paths to learning addressed

Integration

_____ Student-centered lessons
_____ Sophisticated productivity tools
_____ Inquiry, problem solving, and product making in response to a specific task
_____ Higher levels of Bloom's Taxonomy
_____ Three to five paths to learning addressed

Expansion and Refinement

_____ Constructivist methodology
_____ Authentic problem-solving tasks based in real-world experiences
_____ Students have access to all kinds of technology
_____ Higher levels of Bloom's Taxonomy
_____ Five to nine paths to learning addressed

What levels of integration are you currently using? Being aware of your tendencies as a teacher is the first step in addressing all the LoTi levels in your classroom.

Building Bridges Technology Integration

In developing a Building Bridges unit, you will want to be mindful of the LoTi levels of technology integration. While you will want to aspire to Integration and Expansion and Refinement levels, you will find that these are best addressed in the culminating event at the end of your unit. In Learning Tasks, you will be able to generate and select activities that provide for Non-Use, Awareness, Exploration, Infusion, as well as opportunities for Integration and Expansion and Refinement.

Notice that as the levels of integration vary, so do the levels of Bloom and the number of paths to learning that can be addressed. A classroom teacher may be strong at the Infusion level, and that may seem satisfactory. But once you consider that the Infusion level limits students to lower-level thinking and only a few paths to learning at a time, the oneness to branch out and include other levels of technology integration into that classroom becomes more apparent.

Considering LoTi in this light makes a strong case that using technology for its own sake is folly—not simply because of the demands of the Information Age, but because of the need to challenge students at higher levels of thinking across all the modes of human cognition. Consider each of these examples and where they fall on the LoTi scale:

- Taking your class on a virtual field trip through the human circulatory system
- Using Mavis Beacon to practice keyboarding skills
- Creating charts and graphs using data entered into a spreadsheet
- Exploring alternatives to fossil fuel and designing original machines
- Classifying plant samples by observable characteristics
- Creating a digital video of primary source interviews on the Vietnam War

Which lessons make the most of technology, higher-level thinking, and all the paths to learning?

You will want to make use of all of these different kinds of experiences in order for students to successfully participate in units of study. Keep the LoTi levels in mind as you examine each of the sample units offered here, and as you construct your own original units in the future.

Building Understanding:

1. There is a temptation to want to look at the LoTi model as a hierarchy from lower, less desirable levels to higher, more worthy categories. Why is it important not to succumb to this tendency?

2. Why does instructional philosophy play such an important role in the levels of technology integration? Shouldn't it be more a question of teacher proficiency with technology than of instructional style? Why or why not?

3. Reflect on your own technology lessons. At which level of LoTi do you typically find your lessons? Why do you think this is so? What would you need to do to include other LoTi levels in your instructional repertoire?

Chapter 3

The Unit Format:
A Context for Learning

The Big Picture:

The format of the unit design is crucial in creating a context for learning. While there are many suggested unit formats available for teachers, none have combined the elements of recent research on teaching and learning into one effective teaching tool. The unit format presented to you here is an attempt to address these new developments in educational research. Unlike other unit designs, this format is not linear in nature. While the unit is presented here in a deliberate step-by-step manner, it is actually quite open-ended and may be best represented as a Web because there are many different directions it can take. Still, to make the format easy to follow, we will proceed in a linear, logical progression.

Credit for the Building Bridges unit format goes to Heidi Hayes-Jacobs, who originally presented her conceptual unit format 10 years ago. The notion of the conceptual unit is to step back, find the "big picture" concept(s) you wish to teach, and then build your instruction around the concepts rather than the individual skills. It is a very sophisticated model which I have used successfully in my own classroom through the years. Credit likewise goes to Dr. Howard Gardner and his work in multiple intelligences theory, which helped me to develop and maximize this unit format's potential for reaching all of the different learners in the classroom. This unit is also influenced by the work of Dr. Grant Wiggins and Dr. Jay McTighe on backward design, with its emphasis on what is being taught and assessed. Finally, credit goes to Roger Taylor for his inspiring work on integrated, interdisciplinary thematic curriculum units throughout the years, allowing us to begin to see the possibilities for our students. This Building Bridges model has been presented in workshops and at conferences, and further modifications have been made based on feedback from educators around the country. The resulting model offered to you here is the result of all of these influences. It is the format for the units presented in this book.

Standards:

Like all solid instruction, Building Bridges units begin with the identification of standards from each subject area that will be addressed over the course of the unit. For those who work in a self-contained classroom, this may be a straightforward task.

Standards

Theme Mission

Big Idea Learning Tasks

Need to Know Event

Assessment

However, teachers working in a departmentalized setting will need to meet together, each with their own copy of the curriculum and state standards, and identify those indicators they will target. It should not be difficult to identify these objectives, because each seventh-grade teacher already knows his or her discipline: Mr. Jackson and social studies, Mrs. Clemens and science, Mrs. MacDonald and math, Mrs. Bailey and language arts. It is simply a matter of identifying the standards that will be covered successfully by all team members in their respective disciplines. Oftentimes this is the part of unit construction that seems the most like busy work, because you are identifying objectives from lists of standards and stating them explicitly in your unit framework for the sake of sound instructional design. While this may not be the most creative part of the unit writing process, the selection of these objectives is vital, as it sets the guideposts to which everything else must be aligned.

Theme:

With the standards identified, the next step is the selection of the theme of your unit. This should not be a topic, such as the popular dinosaurs, holidays, or oceans. Rather a theme is a broad, all-encompassing idea that indicates the breadth and depth of your unit. It should be applied to all subject areas and create a context for long-lasting understanding. For example, if your unit is going to focus on how independent components can work together to accomplish important tasks, you may wish to choose the theme of Systems for a more scientific emphasis or the theme of Cooperation for a more humanistic tone. Other possible ideas for themes can include, but are not limited to:

Cycles	Frontiers
Networks	Change
Decisions	Goals
Construction	Patterns
Heroes	Choices
Solutions	Standards
Communities	Tools
Boundaries	Conflict
Predictions	Journeys
Senses	Communication

In selecting the theme, you set the tone for the entire unit. On our seventh-grade team, for example, the four teachers will need to compare areas of the curriculum to find similarities, and then agree on one theme that will serve as an umbrella over all subject areas for the duration of the unit. Mr. Jackson teaches the Westward Movement in social studies. Mrs. Clemens, the science teacher, sees possibilities for matching her study of the scientific method with Mr. Jackson's study of the Westward Movement; after all, they both deal with exploring the unknown. Mrs. McDonald sees similar ties for math and her study of solving for an unknown variable in algebra. It's easy for Mrs. Bailey to make connections, as she teaches several novels that cover exploration of unexplored frontiers. After further discussion, the team agrees that Frontiers will be a fruitful theme for them to pursue. They then proceed to meet with their library media specialist, Mrs. Alonzo, who will work with the team to identify traditional and electronic resources to enrich the Frontiers theme. In this way, students can thrive in an environment that accommodates varied paths to learning, even though their classes may be split up amongst several teachers.

Big Idea:

With your theme selected, the next step is to state a big idea that will become the focal point of your unit. A "big idea" is a core concept that is not confined to what students are currently studying. It can be transferred to all kinds of learning experiences and applied to new learning to create new understanding. In short, it is a statement that can be examined using the tools of each subject area. As it is examined from the perspective of each discipline, students gain a deeper understanding of its meaning and, as students move on in their educational careers, it is the big idea that will stay with them as lifelong learners.

Like the theme already selected, a big idea should be broad in its sentiment. It should be rich in meaning, touching on a timeless truth that can be applied across all life experiences, yet reveal itself in layers as students discover new dimensions of its meaning when they explore more deeply. A big idea should be a practical, real-world observation, not a platitude or truism. It can be a familiar quote or an original observation. Whatever you select for your big idea, it will be the standard for your entire unit. Consider these examples:

- Heroes are defined by their circumstances.
- Change is constant.
- Patterns lead us to answers.
- Asking the question requires curiosity; answering the question requires courage.
- On a journey, you must know where you've been and where you're going.
- The best solution saves you time and resources.
- You must define your boundaries before you can encounter others.
- One choice is not as good as another; your criteria determine what is best.
- A network is only as strong as each of its components.
- Building understanding is the key to building community.

Once you have selected a big idea that reveals important characteristics about your theme, it is a good idea to place it on a banner and display it in your room. In this way, the big idea is always visible and easy to refer to as your students explore your theme together.

Need to Know Questions:

With your standards, theme, and big idea in place, the next step in unit building is to generate three to five questions that create a need to know—or a need to find out—in your classroom. Need to know questions are open-ended, "big picture" questions that help students gain a deeper understanding of your big idea. These questions should address broader issues beyond any one subject area and be rich enough in answers that they can be revisited time and time again throughout the unit. Revisiting need to know questions often is an excellent way to keep the focus of the unit in students' minds as they continue their studies. Well-crafted need to know questions often generate even more questions even as they point students toward answers!

Consider the seventh-grade team's Frontiers unit. Here are the need to know questions the team came up with for the students:

- What are the frontiers in our lives?
- Are there frontiers left to explore here on Earth?
- What character traits does it take to explore a frontier?
- Why are we afraid of the unknown?
- What are the rewards of conquering our fears and exploring the unknown?

These questions are designed to keep students coming back for more. While Mr. Jackson asks students to study the perils of settling the old west, Mrs. McDonald is able to address math phobia among her students and support them as they learn new algebraic strategies for problem solving. Mrs. Clemens will use these questions to address setting up proper hypotheses and testing for their veracity through use of the scientific method. And Mrs. Bailey will do character studies of heroes who face the unknown and experience new growth by conquering their fears. In every aspect of the curriculum, these seventh graders will be immersed in the theme of Frontiers and surface with a deeper understanding of how it applies to their own learning and life experience. Once complete, the overview of the unit is in place and it's time to focus on the learning tasks that will support your objectives.

The Mission:

Moments of wonder are born by design. The recollections of educators in Chapter 1 each reveal a climate for truly memorable learning. In the Building Bridges model, the mission is a facilitating event that creates a need for learners to find out more by catching their attention and maintaining their interest. An effective mission immediately engages learners and draws them in to participate in a real-world simulation that includes a problem-solving challenge. This facilitating event not only kicks off unit activities, it creates:

- a purpose for learning
- a climate for learning
- a context for learning

The mission needs to be accomplished within the parameters of the unit by solving a problem or creating a work product that addresses a specific need. A well-crafted mission stimulates the imagination and curiosity of students by empowering them to find ways to respond. The rich, real-world nature of the mission offers students all kinds of choices based on their orientation to learning. Keep in mind that this should be an open-ended task that students will not be able to easily address in a short span of time. Indeed, at the end of the unit, your students may still not have definitive results, but they will have grown dramatically in their understanding of the issues and the processes involved in searching for the answers.

Learning Tasks:

In generating learning tasks in the Building Bridges unit format, there are several constructivist learning theorists to consider. Certainly there is the work of Jean Piaget, Jerome Bruner, and Lev Vygotsky, who each helped define the notion of the learner constructing understanding. Furthermore, there is the work of Robert Sternberg, whose triarchic theory of human intelligence included experiential and contextual aspects of thinking and learning. Finally, there is Howard Gardner's multiple intelligences theory, which espouses at least nine different paths to learning, each with its own identifiable characteristics and functions. While Building Bridges builds upon all these theorists, it generates a range of learning tasks based on nine intelligences.

In considering learning tasks by intelligence, you are forcing yourself to brainstorm ideas that will offer you a wealth of possibilities for instruction by each intelligence. This is not a simple process of conveniently mixing and matching your usual assigned learning tasks to intelligence categories. If that is all you wish to do, why bother designing a new unit at all? You're still going to approach teaching the same way you always have. No, in addressing each intelligence you will need to generate ideas that map back to your standards and align nicely with your task, need to know questions, big idea, and theme.

Mapping means exactly what the term implies: being able to trace a direct path from the beginning to the end of your unit components. Like a road map, if your route does not faithfully take your students to each important stopping point, they will not reach the goals you intend. The standards are the starting point of your map, which should lead you directly to your theme. Your theme should link directly to your big idea. Your big idea should present an obvious context for your need to know questions. Likewise, your questions should point to the task at hand. In short, mapping out a unit using the Building Bridges model helps you create a tight, well-marked road map for your students' learning destination.

But why map learning tasks by intelligence? Don't all the intelligences act in consort? If they don't act in isolation, why plan to teach in isolation? The sole purpose for planning by intelligence is so that you know you have provided activities that cover all the paths to learning. You will not teach the unit in isolated intelligence tasks; you will teach picking and choosing tasks from each intelligence category that effectively address your standards.

In addition to being tied to your objectives, intelligence tasks should be:

- Task-oriented
- Process-based
- Natural (not forced)
- Promoting higher levels of Bloom's Taxonomy
- Adding to the big idea

But how do you identify tasks by intelligence? Consider these descriptors for each intelligence:

Learning Through Language—Verbal/Linguistic
- Read
- Write
- Speak
- Word Study
- Word Games
- Word Puzzles
- Publish Original Work
- Sample Technology: Word Processing

Learning Through Problem Solving—Logical/Mathematical
- Estimate
- Predict
- Reason
- Problem Solving
- Logic Puzzles
- Brain Teasers
- Mysteries
- Sample Technology: Spreadsheet

Learning Through Seeing and Imagining—Visual/Spatial
- Art
- Design
- Map
- Chart
- Graph
- Imagine
- Simulate
- Sample Technology: Digital Camera

Learning Through Patterns—Musical/Rhythmic
- Listen
- Pattern
- Write Poetry
- Chant Rhymes
- Play Music
- Sing Songs
- Listen to Sounds
- Sample Technology: Multimedia Slideshow

Learning Through Interaction with the Environment—Bodily/Kinesthetic
- Build
- Repair
- Perform
- Dance
- Act
- Improvise
- Experiment
- Sample Technology: Assistive Technology Devices

Learning Through Interaction with Others—Interpersonal
- Share
- Discuss
- Collaborate
- Coordinate
- Campaign
- Advertise
- Persuade
- Sample Technology: Online Collaborative Projects

Learning Through Feelings, Values, and Attitudes—Intrapersonal
- Feelings
- Values
- Attitudes
- Standards
- Justice
- Fairness
- Social Issues
- Sample Technology: Digital Portfolios

Learning Through Categories, Hierarchies and Webbing—Naturalist
- Sort
- Filter
- Classify
- Organize
- Categorize
- Identify Attributes
- Build Hierarchies
- Sample Technology: Database

Learning Through Connections to Larger Understandings—Existential
- Ethics
- Aesthetics
- Philosophy
- Existence
- Perspective
- Summarizing

- Community-Building
- Sample Technology: Virtual Field Trips

By mindfully using descriptive verbs for each path to learning, you can develop learning tasks that reach every learner in the classroom.

Culminating Event:

From these nine categories, you can select learning activities that help students to complete the task presented at the outset of the unit. To bring closure to their learning, you will want to design an event that allows learners to show off their responses to that task. The culminating event should be a celebration of learning, a time when those moments of wonder are lofted high for everyone to see. More than just a showcase display, the culminating event is an interactive social event in which other classes, families, and even the community at large are welcomed to participate. A truly successful culminating event will actually transform your classroom into another world, as it takes on the characteristics of your unit of study. A classroom, library, or media center may become an aquarium, an art gallery, or a living museum in which each of your students takes on a role and plays his or her part. At the end of each unit in this book, you will find a suggested culminating activity. You may adapt these ideas to meet your own needs or create original culminating events that are better suited to your environment.

Beyond being a celebration of learning, the culminating event is your optimal opportunity for authentic assessment. Rather than reviewing the attributes of a child's passive work, consider the benefits of assessing a child's learning as he or she interacts with guests, explaining how things work, the principles behind their operation, and the history of their development. Assessing students during a culminating event is a unique opportunity to assess their learning in action. It is the most authentic of assessments.

"But how will I be able to assess each student's work during the culminating event?" you may ask. "Won't I be busy organizing and supervising?" Amazingly, no! While your class' first experience conducting a culminating event will be a learning experience in itself, each student will have a role to play and a location to occupy for the event. And once your guests begin arriving to participate and interact with your students, the entire event takes on a life of its own. Students stay in character because they are engaged and excited about their work. Time moves quickly because of the quality of interaction between your students and invited guests. And behavior problems are non-existent because every child is a valued, featured component of the event. In my own experience, 10 minutes after the event begins, I have been satisfied that everything is moving smoothly and I am free to stand back, observe, and assess.

Of course, you have the choice of either informally observing student mastery or using a formal assessment tool such as a rubric to quantify what you observe. The choice is yours. For me, time was always such a valued commodity as a teacher, I loved being able to complete rubric assessments during the culminating event. It saved me hours of assessment time later on my own.

Assessment:

Because the activities you generate are task-based, process-oriented, and intelligence-centered, you will want to use an authentic assessment tool such as a portfolio, rubric, or checklist in order to measure student success in meeting the stated objectives of the unit. These tools should include criteria that evaluate the student's role in the class culminating event. Did the student stay in character? Was his or her apparel appropriate for the role? Did he or she present work products with a certain level of expertise? Was technology used appropriately and effectively? How did he or she handle questions from his or her audience?

Each unit included in the book contains rubrics that assess student participation and work products. In the final chapter, we will discuss rubric construction and provide you with the tools you need to develop assessment rubrics for your own original multiple intelligence units.

✚ Building Understanding:

1. What are your intelligence strengths? Do you teach to these strengths? How well do you teach to the intelligences that are not your strengths?

2. Why is it important that the standards, theme, big idea, need to know questions, task, intelligences, and the culminating event all align to one another? What are the implications for student success?

3. The culminating event of your unit should provide rich opportunities for assessment of student learning. How can you design a culminating event so that assessment is accurate and effective?

Chapter $\boxed{4}$

Build a Classroom

Space Colony

This Frontiers unit challenges students to consider the frontiers that lay ahead for planet Earth. Pick and choose from the suggested activities provided here and add your own ideas to create a tailor-made memorable learning experience, as your children set out to build a space colony on the planet Mars!

AGE: Elementary School, but can be adapted to any grade level

Standards:

National English Language Arts Standards—
NCTE/IRA National Council of Teachers of English (2001).

1. Read a wide range of print and non-print texts to build an understanding of texts, of themselves, and of the cultures of the United States and the world; to acquire new information; to respond to the needs and demands of society and the workplace; and for personal fulfillment. Among these texts are fiction and nonfiction, classic and contemporary works.

2. Adjust use of spoken, written, and visual language (e.g., conventions, style, vocabulary) to communicate effectively with a variety of audiences and for different purposes.

3. Use a variety of technological and information resources (e.g., libraries, databases, computer networks, video) to gather and synthesize information and to create and communicate knowledge.

Standards for the English Language Arts, by the International Reading Association and the National Council of Teachers of English, Copyright 1996 by the International Reading Association and the National Council of Teachers of English. Reprinted with permission.

National Mathematics Standards—
NCTM National Council of Teachers of Mathematics (2000).

1. Use visualization, spatial reasoning, and geometric modeling to solve problems.
2. Understand measurable attributes of objects and the units, systems, and processes of measurement.
3. Apply appropriate techniques, tools, and formulas to determine measurements.
4. Apply and adapt a variety of appropriate strategies to solve problems.
5. Communicate their mathematical thinking coherently and clearly to peers, teachers, and others.
6. Understand how mathematical ideas interconnect and build on one another to produce a coherent whole.
7. Recognize and apply mathematics in contexts outside of mathematics.
8. Use representations to model and interpret physical, social, and mathematical phenomena.

Standards are listed with the permission of the National Council of Teachers of Mathematics (NCTM). NCTM does not endorse the content or validity of these alignments.

National Science Standards—
NAS National Academy of Science (1995).

1. Form and function are complementary aspects of objects, organisms, and systems in the natural and designed world.

Reprinted with permission from "What Is the Influence of the National Science Education Standards?: Reviewing the Evidence, A Workshop Summary" (2003) by the National Academy of Sciences, courtesy of the National Academies Press, Washington, D.C.

National Social Studies Standards—
NCSS National Council for the Social Studies (1997).

1. Human beings create, learn, and adapt culture.
2. People have wants that often exceed the limited resources available to them.
3. Technology forms the basis for some of our most difficult social choices.

Permission to reprint standards granted by the National Council of Social Studies Publications.

THEME: *Frontiers*

 Big Idea: Exploring the unknown requires courage, an open mind, and the ability to adapt.

 Need to Know Questions:

1. What are the frontiers of the 21st century?
2. Why do we have a fear of the unknown?
3. What qualities do we need to explore the unknown?
4. How does the scientific method help explore the unknown?
5. How does creative problem solving help explore the unknown?

 Mission:

Read the following press release to the class:

> "<u>FOR IMMEDIATE RELEASE</u>: Volunteers wanted to explore the surface of Mars and create the first human colony there. All supplies to build a viable space colony will be provided. This is a lifetime commitment with many unanswered questions and rewards. The faint of heart should not apply! All interested parties should contact NASA with a resume of appropriate qualities for settling this new frontier.

Ask the class to brainstorm the qualities necessary to successfully explore a new frontier. Create a chart of these qualities and post it in the classroom. Announce to the class that you would like students to pursue this challenge and help explore this new frontier for humankind. Have each student create a resume that highlights his or her strong qualifications for becoming an explorer and colonist of Mars.

 Learning Tasks:

 Learning Through Language

- Read a book about a frontier. Have students examine closely the characteristics that make the setting for a book about the frontier. Conduct a character study to identify the qualities of the characters in the book that make it possible to live on the frontier.
- Write an autobiographical anecdote about a memory of being alone in an unfamiliar place. Use descriptive words to relate the experience to the reader. What kinds of thoughts did you have? What kinds of emotions did you feel?
- Formulate and agree upon rules for a space colony. Once you have a consensus on the rules, conduct a formal signing ceremony and then post the rules for all to see within your classroom.

- Make parchment paper and write contracts, deeds, and treaties for your colony. Stress the use of business vocabulary that stipulates ownership, responsibilities, agreements, and enforcement of terms for each document.

- Brainstorm descriptive words and phrases for a territory and write poetry describing it. Work your way up to writing descriptive poetry about the Martian landscape. Emphasize concrete poetry that is free of rhyme scheme so that students can focus on word selection and the images and emotions that are evoked.

- Write fictional accounts about life in a space colony. Consider publishing these accounts in newspaper format for the class to publish and share. Include advertisements of items that would be in demand when living in the space colony, as well as weather, sports, and lifestyle columns.

- Create original words describing your space colony; review the meaning of prefixes and suffixes by adjoining them to imaginary words; have students define their words and create pronunciation keys for a class dictionary of original frontier adjectives.

- Make videotaped recruiting advertisements for joining the Mars space colony. Use different techniques of persuasion to encourage people to join. Include opportunity for students to create costumes and props and let them rehearse before actually filming their ads.

- Publish a brochure or flyer that advertises the benefits of living in your space colony. Include catchy slogans and attention-grabbing headlines that entice Earth-dwellers to want to come live with you in space.

- Develop a class PowerPoint presentation in which each student contributes one or more slides about his or her role in the space colony. Use each role as the starting point for discussing student roles in the culminating event for the unit.

- Host a class Web page that allows visitors to see your imaginary space colony in action. Include logs of activities you complete and data you collect. Original student writing and artwork can help to set your Web site apart from all others online!

Learning Through Problem Solving

- Introduce variables as the "unknown" in mathematics; practice ways of solving for a variable in simple arithmetic sentences. Allow students to share the different strategies they use for coming up with a right answer. Test each strategy as a group to make sure that it is mathematically sound.

- Participate in a simulation that requires travel over time, record keeping of supplies, problem solving, estimation, and use of time and money to reach the space colony alive. This can be done over a period of days, regularly announcing to students when they have reached a new point in space, when they grow short on supplies, and when new supplies are acquired. Each student can keep track of the information in a space travel notebook.

- Ask students to determine their weights on Mars, as well as the weights of many of the common household items they will be using while in the space colony. Use a table or spreadsheet to list the items and their weights on both Mars and Earth so that students can make comparisons.

- Estimate distances, areas, volumes, and masses of the space colony using agreed upon units of measure. This can include original agreed upon units of measure that your students create. Explore the issue of a standardized unit of measure and why it is so important in scientific inquiry.

- Map out your space colony to scale. Begin by having the class plan a classroom space colony, making use of your existing classroom furniture. Then have students draw a map of the proposed layout of the colony on a sheet of paper using an agreed-upon scale to represent items in your classroom.

- On the completed map, use map grids to divide the space colony into equal portions; then make different sized grids of the colony so that students can appreciate how scale allows items to remain in proportion regardless of the size of the map.

- Measure the school building floor plan in meters and create a small scale of the school layout. Determine whether a replica of your school building could be built inside your space colony. Design the space colony school, based on your class's recommendations and then have the class use available materials to build a model of the school.

- Complete a WebQuest to a new frontier, or have your class devise a WebQuest about successfully pioneering a space colony on Mars. Make sure the student work product that results from the WebQuest will emphasize the exploration of Mars as a new frontier.

- Research data on Mars and Earth: temperature, climate, seasons, length of day, length of year, minerals, and raw materials. Place the data into a spreadsheet and compare it with data on Earth. Use the spreadsheet's chart and graph capability to make pictorial representations of the data.

- Discuss common emergencies that may occur in the space colony. Have students flow chart the proper procedures for handling these emergencies. Bring these flow charts together into a policy manual to be kept on hand in the colony.

Learning Through Seeing and Imagining

- Survey the art of the American colonies and the westward expansion to determine how our ancestors viewed their frontiers. Create a wall display in your classroom of these different representations of frontiers. Allow students the opportunity to create sketches of these different pictures.

- Study images of the international space station and identify the key components for building a space colony. Use household materials to build a 3-D model of the class's proposed space station.

- Use student-generated figures on the dimensions of the proposed space colony and mark off the actual size and shape of the proposed colony on the playground using string or chalk.

- Use drawing or painting software to allow students to create a visual representation of the space colony on the computer. Save each digital drawing so that you have a collection of visual representations of the space colony.

- Design signs, graphics, and artwork for the space colony. This would include labels for common items and rooms, safety signs, directional signs, and signs that label each student's personal quarters in the space colony.
- Compare the different techniques illustrators use to represent frontiers in children's literature. Encourage students to make their own frontier sketches based on the titles they are reading during the unit.
- Study photographs of the Martian surface; discuss color, shape, texture, and perspective in the different images. Become familiar with a specific Martian landscape where your class would like its space colony to be built.
- Use a variety of media to illustrate the landscape of Mars. Emphasize to the students that they must be faithful in representing the colors and textures of the Martian surface, as they have studied it in photographs.
- Scan images of Mars so that they can be saved in digital format. Then allow students to open up Mars photographs in a draw or paint program and add detail to the pictures, such as inserting a drawing of the space colony, including their images in the landscape, and adding labels to specific points of interest in the photograph.
- Use graphics editing software to manipulate and combine elements from different digital pictures of Mars into new composite images. This can include other digital images students have already created and original artwork that has been scanned into a usable digital format.
- Create an original space video using digital images and editing software, or by filming actual objects with a digital video camera. Allow students to dub in voice narration, sound effects, and music to enhance the experience of watching the video.

❖ Learning Through Patterns

- Listen to space age music while working on the space colony. Point out the strategies musicians use to create a frontier atmosphere in their compositions.
- Listen to sounds from space and identify patterns and repetitions that you hear. Keep a collection of digital audio sounds that can be imported into digital work products.
- Identify patterns on the Martian surface and generate predictions about what the surface is like. Have students create a larger view of the surface by repeating patterns in a digital draw or paint program.
- Encourage movement to sounds and music about space. You may wish to let students move to sound silently or to narrate an imagined sequence of events as they listen to music or sound, and then move accordingly to act out the story.
- Listen to music from the age of exploration, colonies, and frontiers. Discuss how the music captures the characteristics of the unknown. Compare music from past ages with music composed today on a frontiers theme.
- Listen to songs about frontiers in life. Discuss the imagery in the lyrics. Point out metaphor, simile, and allegory. Create a class top 40 list of favorite frontiers lyrics.
- Write poetry that describes the characteristics of a frontier, using rhyme schemes that help convey the feel of the unknown. Allow students to be creative and use unconventional rhyming patterns.

- Write free form poetry that makes use of vibrant adjectives to describe the qualities of an explorer.
- Design and build instruments which make unique sounds that will be heard in the space colony. Use household materials and allow students to develop their own original instruments.
- Compose an original musical score that makes use of original student instruments.
- Create a digital recording of original music scores that can be added to student work products.

Learning Through Interaction with the Environment

- Make original space costumes to wear in the colony using available materials.
- Fashion space colony tools from common household items.
- Use simple machines to construct complex machines that will do work for students in the space colony.
- Build a fitness course to help prepare students for life in a space colony.
- Have students complete the fitness trail on a regular basis as part of their space colony training.
- Build scale models of the space station using common household materials. Have students refer to their map designs in order to make sure their models are to scale.
- Use clay or papier-mâché to create small models of the Martian surface. Have students pay attention to the color and texture of their work.
- Conduct experiments on rocks and soil in preparation for tests of the Martian surface. Learn how to identify different classes of rocks based on your experiments.
- Build a model of a space shuttle that will be used to transport the class to Mars. Include all the necessary supplies that will be stored in the cargo bay.
- Have students use flight simulator software to practice flying and landing aircraft

Learning Through Interaction with Others

- Have students write to government agencies, e-mail Ask an Expert services, contact NASA, collect news items, view documentaries, and use the Internet to gather resources on exploring space.
- Break the class into teams of four or five and conduct team-building activities in preparation for their work in the space colony.
- Identify a dilemma in space (virus, contamination, drought, equipment malfunction) and collaborate in teams to solve the problem.
- Invite a NASA astronaut to visit your class and discuss proper training for space travel.
- Act out imaginary activities around a space colony campfire. Have students stay in character to maintain an authentic experience.
- Act out an improvisation charting the Martian frontier: how do we explore? Who leads? What will be done if we encounter others? Is there a manifest destiny to this territory?
- Develop an economic system for a frontier, which is not based on paper money, that will allow colonists to buy and sell goods and services as they are needed. Generate enough of the currency to be used in a classroom rewards system during the unit.

- Design a space colony exhibit with jobs that include ticket persons, tour guides, security persons, aerospace experts, Mars experts, speakers, sales people, and maintenance people. Have students stay in character while inviting other classes to see your exhibit.
- Use an instant messenger application from a remote location and simulate text-based communication between Mars space colonists and scientists here on Earth.
- Collaborate via e-mail with a class (or classes) from another nation. Work together to plan how all nations of Earth will share in the colonization of Mars.

♥ Learning Through Feelings, Values, and Attitudes

- NASA responds to our class application that only a certain number of students will be able to travel to the space colony. Others will stay here on Earth to help with the mission from here. How will we decide who gets to go and who stays? Develop a list of fair criteria.
- How will duties and chores be divided in the space colony? Create a process that determines who does what.
- Research the "code of the West" and compare it to modern day criminal law. What kind of law will be needed in a space colony?
- Perform daily journal writing that responds to the space colony activities in the classroom.
- Create a questionnaire and survey other classes on their feelings and attitudes about colonizing space. Analyze the results and compare them with survey results from your own class.
- Develop a class policy statement on the colonization of space and how it will affect life here on Earth. Present it to local lawmakers or publish it in the local newspaper.
- Have a class debate. Once you arrive in the space colony, is it realistic to ever expect to come back to Earth?
- Conduct a mock election for leaders of the space colony; develop issues and platforms for two to three candidates and conduct a debate. Conclude the process with a secret ballot vote.
- Introduce a creative problem-solving task. You are short on food for the month and you have lost contact with Mission Control on Earth. You need to regain contact or find a way to survive on your own until the next shuttle arrives with deliveries. What will you do? Determine criteria for a best solution and then brainstorm possible solutions that can be compared against your criteria to identify the best possible solution.
- Have each student perform a self-assessment on his or her work in this unit.

Learning Through Categories, Hierarchies, and Webbing

- Identify and label every room and its function in the space colony. Transfer these labels onto all space colony maps and models.
- Learn the different ranks and levels of command for NASA astronauts and apply them to roles in the space colony.
- Categorize different jobs in the space colony by agreed upon attributes. Make sure everyone has a role.
- Employ semantic mapping software to create a visual hierarchy of the space colony that shows everyone's roles in the classroom.
- Use microscopes, telescopes, and sample collection kits for use in the space colony.
- Practice using the scientific method in looking for answers to questions about living on Mars.
- Design a classification system for identifying rocks, soil, minerals, fossils, and forms of life found on Mars.
- Sketch imaginary fossilized Martian animals. Construct life-sized models of the animals using everyday materials.
- Keep a digital scrapbook of classroom activities about the space colony. Make use of a digital camera to capture activities and memorable moments as they occur.
- Compile data about Mars and your space colony into a database and have students practice conducting queries to find data on your space colony.

Learning Through Connections to Larger Understanding

- Visit a planetarium and experience the solar system through a presentation.
- Design a mission patch for your class's space colony. Produce enough copies of it that everyone can wear it as part of their space colony uniform.
- Devise symbols that can be understood across language barriers in the space colony. Make a chart explaining each symbol and its meaning.

- Create a diorama of a Martian landscape.
- Construct a wall-sized physical map of a Martian landscape.
- Take a virtual field trip to Mars using existing Web sites available online that contain Mars data and images.
- Create a space colony virtual field trip using digital pictures of your students' work. Post it on your school Web site so that visitors can participate in your space colony vicariously.
- Participate in a virtual community that discusses the work being done in space.
- Keep records of discussions your class has while chatting online.
- Investigate the possibilities for life on Mars. Have students publish their findings online.
- Convert your classroom into a working model of a Mars space colony in anticipation of the culminating event.

Culminating Event:

Transform the classroom into a space colony. Bring together all of the different work products students have completed to make the space colony a showcase of student accomplishments. Have students take on roles in the space colony so that they can serve as experts on what they have learned. Invite other classes, parents, and the outside community to come in and visit your space colony on one designated day.

 Resources:

 Books

Primary

> *A Dark, Dark Tale* by Ruth Brown
> *Finding Providence: The Story of Roger Williams* by Avi
> *The Flood That Came to Grandma's House* by Joan Schooley
> *How Much Is a Million?* by Stephen Kellogg
> *Moonwalk: the First Trip to the Moon* by Judy Donnelly
> *Prairie Visions* by Pam Conrad
> *Tattie's River Journey* by Shirley Murphy
> *Trapped by the Ice: Shackleton's Amazing Antarctic Adventure* by Michael McCurdy
> *The Very Hungry Caterpillar* by Eric Carle
> *We're Going on a Bear Hunt* by Michael Rosen
> *The World that Jack Built* by Ruth Brown

Elementary

> *Bad Day at Riverbend* by Chris Van Allsburg
> *Caddie Woodlawn* by Carol Brink
> *Hatchet* by Gary Paulsen
> *If You Made a Million?* by Stephen Kellogg
> *I Have Heard of a Land* by Joyce Thomas
> *My Prairie Year: Based on the Diary of Elenore Plaisted* by Brett Harvey
> *Sacagawea* by Judith St. George
> *Sign of the Beaver* by Elizabeth George Speare
> *Trouble River* by Betsy Byars
> *Wagon Wheels* by Barbara Brenner

Middle School

> *Alien Secrets* by Annette Klause
> *Alone Across the Arctic: One Woman's Epic Journey By Dog Team*
>   by Pam Flowers and Ann Dixon
> *The Borning Room* by Paul Fleischman
> *Columbus and the World Around Him* by Milton Meltzer
> *Commodore Perry in the Land of the Shogun* by Rhoda Blumberg
> *Hero and the Crown* by Robin McKinley
> *Hiroshima No Pika* by Toshi Maruki
> *The Light in the Forest* by Conrad Richter

Prairie Visions by Pam Conrad
A River Ran Wild by Lynn Cherry
Weasel by Cynthia DeFelice

High School

All Quiet on the Western Front by Erich Maria Remarque
Cosmos by Carl Sagan
Cowboy Ghost by Robert Newton Peck
Daughter of Fortune by Isabel Allende
The Endurance: Shackleton's Legendary Antarctic Expedition
    by Caroline Alexander
The Grapes of Wrath by John Steinbeck
Gravity by Tess Gerritsen
The Innocents Within by Robery Daley
Journey to the Center of the Earth by Jules Verne
On the Road by Jack Kerouac
Twenty Thousand Leagues Under the Seas by Jules Verne

Music

Cool Change—Little River Band
Album: Greatest Hits

Dead Heart—Midnight Oil
Album: Diesel and Dust

Farewell to Tarwathie—Judy Collins
Album: Colors of the Day

Games without Frontiers—Peter Gabriel
Album: Peter Gabriel

Imagine—John Lennon
Album: Imagine

Orinoco Flow (Sail Away)—Enya
Album: Watermark

Roam—B52s
Album: Cosmic Thing

Rocket Man—Elton John
Album: Honky Chateau

Sweet Surrender—John Denver
Album: Back Home Again

Up Around the Bend—Creedence Clearwater Revival
Album: Chronicle

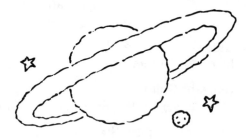

@ Web Resources

Amazing Space
<http://amazing-space.stsci.edu/>

Ask a High Energy Astronomer
<http://imagine.gsfc.nasa.gov/docs/ask_astro/ask_an_astronomer.html>

Ask Dr. Universe
<http://www.wsu.edu/DrUniverse/>

Brain Warp
<http://www.spaceday.org/conmgmt/index.php?option=displaypage&Itemid=60&op
=page&SubMenu=>

Challenging the Space Frontier
<http://teacher.scholastic.com/space/index.htm>

Exploratorium Magazine Online
<http://www.exploratorium.edu/exploring/space/index.html>

Exploring Mars
<http://www.exploringmars.com/>

Exploring Planets in the Classroom
<http://www.spacegrant.hawaii.edu/class_acts/index.html>

Frontier House
<http://www.pbs.org/wnet/frontierhouse/>

Frontiers
<http://www.pparc.ac.uk/frontiers/>

Glossary of NASA Acronyms and Abbreviations
<http://science.ksc.nasa.gov/shuttle/technology/sts-newsref/stsover-acronyms.html>

Hands-On Universe
<http://hou.lbl.gov/>

Intelligent Child
<http://www.intelligentchild.com/index.html>

International Space Station
<http://spaceflight.nasa.gov/station/>

International Space Station by Discovery.com
<http://www.discovery.com/stories/science/iss/iss.html>

K–8 Aeronautics
<http://wings.avkids.com/>

Kids' Space
<http://www.kids-space.org/>

Johnson Space Center Digital Image Collection
<http://images.jsc.nasa.gov/>

Mars Academy
<http://www.marsacademy.com/>

Mars Millennium Project
<http://www.mars2030.net/>

Mars Missions: Past, Present, and Future
<http://mars.sgi.com/>

Mars Pathfinder
<http://mars.jpl.nasa.gov/default.html>

Mars Pathfinder Project Information
<http://nssdc.gsfc.nasa.gov/planetary/mesur.html>

Mars Pathfinder Spacecraft Model!
<http://mpfwww.jpl.nasa.gov/mpf/education/cutouts.html>

Mars Team Online
<http://quest.arc.nasa.gov/mars/>

Martian Driver's License
<http://mpfwww.jpl.nasa.gov/mpf/education/drivlic.html>

Mission to Mars
<http://library.thinkquest.org/11147/>

NASA Human Space Flight
<http://spaceflight.nasa.gov/>

NASA Kids
<http://kids.msfc.nasa.gov/>

NASA Quest
<http://quest.arc.nasa.gov/>

NASA Spacelink
<http://spacelink.nasa.gov/.index.html>

NASA Student Involvement Project
<http://www.nsip.net/index.cfm>

NASA Television Coverage on the Internet
<http://btree-esn.grc.nasa.gov/NASA_TV/NASA_TV.html>

The Nine Planets
<http://seds.lpl.arizona.edu/nineplanets/nineplanets/nineplanets.html>

Origins of the Universe
<http://origins.jpl.nasa.gov/>

Passport to Knowledge
<http://passporttoknowledge.com/students.html>

Pioneer Life in America
<http://library.thinkquest.org/J001587/>

Planetary Geology
<http://spacelink.nasa.gov/Instructional.Materials/NASA.Educational.Products/
Planetary.Geology/>

Planetary Photojournal

<http://photojournal.jpl.nasa.gov/>

Sample Sounds from Space
<http://spaceweather.com/glossary/inspire.html>

Sounds of Space Weather
<http://www.spaceweathersounds.com/>

Space Place
<http://spaceplace.jpl.nasa.gov/>

Space Weather
<http://www.windows.ucar.edu/spaceweather/index.html>

Star Child
<http://starchild.gsfc.nasa.gov/docs/StarChild/StarChild.html>

TeachSPACE
<http://www.space.com/teachspace/>

Virtual Tour into the Universe
<http://library.thinkquest.org/28327/>

Windowpane Observatory
<http://www.wpo.net/>

Featured Software Title

Adobe PhotoShop
<http://www.adobe.com/products/photoshop/main.html>

Photoshop remains the industry standard graphics editor. Utilizing the power of Photoshop in your classroom, students can create, manipulate, and manage images to help them become highly productive users of technology.

✚ *Building Understanding:*

1. What national, state, and local standards can be addressed in the Frontiers unit?

2. What local resources to which you have access would further enrich the Frontiers unit?

3. What criteria would you add to the participation rubric for evaluating each student's participation in the culminating event?

 *Assessment:*

Figure 4.1—Frontiers Unit Participation Rubric

Participation	Needs Improvement 1	Satisfactory 2	Exemplary 3
Participates in class activities.	Occasionally when interested in the task.	Regularly whenever prompted to join.	Consistently with interest and enthusiasm.
Cooperates with peers.	Depends on whom he or she is working with.	Shares and works cooperatively.	Serves as a role model for sharing and cooperating.
Is a collaborative partner.	Does not share ideas or does not listen to others.	Collaborates to successfully complete tasks.	Is a class leader in forming collaborative partnerships.
Demonstrates characteristics of an explorer.	Does not like to take risks or explore unknown subject matter.	Takes risks and seeks support to explore the unknown.	Takes risks, seeks support, and uses critical-thinking skills to explore the unknown.
Demonstrated mastery of skills specified in state standards.	Did not meet the minimum requirements for state standards targeted in this unit.	Met the minimum requirements for state standards targeted in this unit.	Exceeded the minimum requirements for state standards targeted in this unit.

Figure 4.2—Frontiers Unit Project Rubric

Project	Needs Improvement 1	Satisfactory 2	Exemplary 3
Is done neatly with attention to detail.	Project is incomplete or lacks sufficient depth.	Project is neat and shows attention to detail.	Project is neat, shows attention to detail, and exhibits craftsmanship that goes beyond grade-level expectations
Is based in an identified content area of the unit.	Is not related to any content area being studied under the theme of frontiers.	Is based in one identified content area.	Is based in two or more identified content areas.
Applies skills and concepts in a new or different way.	Project imitates objects or examples studied in class.	Project demonstrates mastery of skills and concepts in a unique way.	Project demonstrates mastery of skills and concepts in a unique way at the highest level of thinking.
Adds to the class study of frontiers.	Does not add to the class experience or understanding of frontiers.	Adds to the class understanding of frontiers or explorers.	Adds to the class understanding of frontiers or explorers by elevating the level of discussion or activity.
Demonstrated high personal standards for work.	Does not demonstrate high personal standards in the completion of the project.	Demonstrates high standards for work as outlined by the teacher and/or class.	Demonstrates high personal standards for work that exceeds teacher expectations.

Chapter 5

Become

Time Travelers

T his Changes unit engages students to become travelers and predict what life will be like in years to come. The culminating event is a time traveling museum in which each learner takes part in interactive displays that share students' understandings of change and time!

AGE: Middle School, but can be adapted to any grade level

Standards:

National English Language Arts Standards—
NCTE/IRA National Council of Teachers of English (2001).

1. Read a wide range of print and non-print texts to build an understanding of texts, of themselves, and of the cultures of the United States and the world; to acquire new information; to respond to the needs and demands of society and the workplace; and for personal fulfillment. Among these texts are fiction and nonfiction, classic and contemporary works.

2. Read a wide range of literature from many periods in many genres to build an understanding of the many dimensions (e.g., philosophical, ethical, aesthetic) of human experience.

3. Employ a wide range of strategies as they write and use different writing process elements appropriately to communicate with different audiences for a variety of purposes.

4. Develop an understanding of and respect for diversity in language use, patterns, and dialects across cultures, ethnic groups, geographic regions, and social roles.

Standards for the English Language Arts, by the International Reading Association and the National Council of Teachers of English, Copyright 1996 by the International Reading Association and the National Council of Teachers of English. Reprinted with permission.

National Mathematics Standards—
NCTM National Council of Teachers of Mathematics (2000).

1. Understand numbers, ways of representing numbers, relationships among numbers, and number systems.
2. Understand patterns, relations, and functions.
3. Analyze change in various contexts.
4. Select and use appropriate statistical methods to analyze data.
5. Analyze and evaluate the mathematical thinking and strategies of others.
6. Create and use representations to organize, record, and communicate mathematical ideas.

Standards are listed with the permission of the National Council of Teachers of Mathematics (NCTM). NCTM does not endorse the content or validity of these alignments.

National Science Standards—
NAS National Academy of Science (1995).

1. Types and levels of organization provide useful ways of thinking about the world.

Reprinted with permission from "What Is the Influence of the National Science Education Standards?: Reviewing the Evidence, A Workshop Summary" (2003) by the National Academy of Sciences, courtesy of the National Academies Press, Washington, D.C.

National Social Studies Standards—
NCSS National Council for the Social Studies (1997).

1. Personal identity is shaped by one's culture, by groups, and by institutional influences.

Permission to reprint standards granted by the National Council of Social Studies Publications.

THEME: *Change*

! **Big Idea:** Everything changes.

? **Need to Know Questions:**

1. Does anything stay the same?
2. What causes change?
3. Is change a good thing?
4. Why don't people like change?
5. How can we measure change?

★ **Mission:**

Conduct this creative visualization exercise with your class:

Have students close their eyes and focus in on your voice. Tell them you are taking them back in time to the era when people were first settling your state.

Ask them to picture in their minds what the state looked like before it was first settled. Describe the kinds of physical features they might have seen as they continue to close their eyes, listen, and imagine.

Now ask them to continue to keep their eyes closed and imagine themselves standing in your state at the time of the Civil War. Ask them to imagine how the state looks differently from the time it was first settled. Remind them to be quiet and not to respond out loud, but to continue envisioning themselves traveling through time.

Ask them to continue to keep their eyes closed and to focus on your voice as they now imagine themselves standing in your state during the Great Depression. Describe what they might be able to see as they create the images in their minds. Remind them to compare your state during the time of the Depression with those times you have already visited in your mind.

Finally, ask your students to imagine themselves standing in your state today. Ask them to imagine the things that have changed and the ways life goes on around them differently. Describe specific changes they may notice in comparison to times past. When you are done, give students a minute to finish their visual exercise and then gently ask them to open their eyes and rejoin you in the classroom.

Ask students to share what they notice changed over time as you traveled together through your use of imagination. Note not only what changed, but why it changed. Discuss how your state and the world around it have changed over time. Invite your students to become time travelers who will further investigate why things change and why they cannot stay the same.

Learning Tasks:

Learning Through Language

- Share literature from each century of American history. Look at each title chronologically and discuss the changes in theme, style, and content over time.
- Examine significant documents in American history. Make use of online collections of primary sources and create an archive in your classroom.
- Recite excerpts from American poetry, literature, and speeches. Have each student create a digital collection of his or her favorite historic poetry and prose.
- Assign small groups to research specific periods in American history. Have each group create a cache of resources that reflect the popular culture of the time period.

  - Have students keep time traveler's journals, creating original accounts of everyday life. Students may opt to write about the time period they are researching in their small groups.
  - Interview older citizens to learn the oral history of your area. Use audiotape or digital cameras to capture the interviews so they can be reviewed by the class and shared online.
  - Describe observed changes in simulations and experiments observed in class. Emphasize the necessity to use accurate, descriptive terms in order to create vivid accounts of what is observed.

- Write a biographical account of a state hero. Students may choose to write in the first, second, or third person. Require research before students begin to write.
- Create original adverbs and adjectives that describe how things change. Review the rules of grammar for adverbs and adjectives so that students will create original terms that follow the conventions of proper English.
- Publish a class newspaper in which each section focuses on a different era of American or state history.

Learning Through Problem Solving

- Create a timeline of significant events in your state's history. You may opt to create the timeline as successive slides in a slideshow or using an application like Timeliner.
- Design a flow chart that describes the steps in the change process. Have the class agree on one best flow chart that will be displayed in the room as a visual reminder.
- Explore ways to measure change. Have students come up with their own ideas that they can test and analyze. Have the class select the best ways to measure change.
- Practice measuring elapsed time. Use records of events that last over a period of days and have students determine the time that has elapsed between successive events.
- Analyze significant inventions in American history and how they helped change the way we live. Have students examine life before and after the introduction of an invention into everyday American life.
- Study and project population patterns over the past century. Use data from U.S. government census figures to help determine trends in growth.

- Examine trends in immigration from 1700 through today. Have students make projections for the next 50 years based on the patterns they perceive.
- Compare life expectancies in this country from 1670, 1770, 1870, 1970, and today. Research the major causes of death at each point in time. Draw conclusions as to what has changed in quality of life.
- Compare units of measurement used in the 1700s and today. Determine how we agreed upon the current U.S. standards and why we do not use the metric system.
- Study timepieces used from the 1600s through today. Include analog and digital clocks and watches.

◎ Learning Through Seeing and Imagining

- Sketch examples of American symbols showing how they have changed over time.
- Know your state and national flags as they have evolved over time. Have students sketch each flag as it has changed.
- Map how our nation's political geography has changed over time. Use overhead transparencies and create overlays that show political growth and change.
- Map your state's political geography in 1700, 1800, 1900, and today. Create the state map in a slideshow, where each successive slide reflects new growth within a century.
- Diagram everyday clothing worn in 1620, 1720, 1820, 1920, and today. Ask your local historical society if they have examples of actual garments from each century you can examine.
- Study American landscape paintings from each century and note the differences in style. Try to find paintings of the same landscape from different time periods to compare perspective and change.
- Compare American portraits painted over time, noting the differences in style. Have students create self-portraits in the style of different centuries.
- Collect pictures of your town or state. Organize them into a digital scrapbook that you can share with the community on your school Web site.
- Design the layout for a time traveler's museum that would fit in your classroom. Agree on the plan as a class.
- Design signs and graphics for a time traveler's museum. Include labels, directions, and safety messages.

◆ Learning Through Patterns

- Sing songs of each era in American history. Study the historical context of each song.
- Move to music from each era. Learn the dances that were popular in each period of time.
- Clap to the rhythm of American folk songs. Have students compare the different pacing of songs.

- Listen to songs about change. Include songs from the 1960s that reflect the social unrest of that era.
- Study musical instruments created over time. Note especially the way changes in technology have impacted the creation of new kinds of instruments.
- Create instruments from each era of American history that make sounds you can hear in your community.
- Write poems about changes that have a rhyme scheme that changes as the poem plays itself out.
    - Identify recurring patterns in American history. Compare and contrast two major events in American history that play out a similar pattern.
    - Identify recurring kinds of change. Share examples of how specific kinds of change occur in our lives today.
    - Predict a future change based on the patterns your class has studied. Have each student predict a future social or historical event based on his or her research.

Learning Through Interaction with the Environment

- Demonstrate the concept of change using nonverbal gestures. The student may perform in any way he or she chooses, but cannot use language to aid in communicating the change.
- Act out examples of cause and effect. Students may select partners to help them demonstrate the concept.
- Take a walking tour of your town. Have students use digital cameras and sketch pads to capture images and make notes on what they see.
- Build models of historic buildings in your community. Create a scale model of your downtown district.
- Create 3-D topographical maps of your state showing how the land has changed over time.
- Play with toys or games from each century of American history. Discuss how children's recreation has changed over time. Note especially the changes technology has facilitated.
- Conduct simulations and experiments that demonstrate change taking place. Allow students to handle the materials and manipulate variables in conducting the tasks.
- Invent timepieces using household materials that can keep time accurately.
- Design costumes for each period of American history. Allow students the option of creating their own period-specific costumes as part of their research.
- Build time traveler museum displays. Have each student create at least one display showing off his or her work.

Learning Through Interaction with Others

- Interview experts on state history. Keep a record of the interview either digitally or in hard copy.
- Study communication as it has evolved since your state was first settled. Note changes that have occurred over time.

- Create a class ask-an-expert service on state history. Post it online and have students take turns responding to inquiries from around your state.
- Communicate with a class from another state to compare how change has taken place in both localities.
- Examine how the manners of society have changed over time. Have students create a list of etiquette from each century.
- Make a persuasive argument for preserving or changing a landmark. Send it to your local newspaper's editorial staff.
- Work in groups to plan a time traveler museum. Work as a class to implement each group's plan as part of a comprehensive exhibit.
- Assign jobs for a time traveler museum. Have each student develop a character and costume for his or her role.
- Create displays for a time traveler museum in which each student interacts with visitors to share his or her work.
- Create a quiz show in which visitors to your time traveler museum can participate.

♥ Learning Through Feelings, Values, and Attitudes

- Study old and existing laws in your state and discuss why they were enacted, and (if they are still on the books) why they exist and why they are or are not enforced.
- Study a significant American election in which citizens asked for change at the voting booth. Identify the feelings and values of the voters at that time which resulted in that vote.
- Imagine how your state may change in the future so that it can preserve its past and change to accommodate new growth.
- Devise a plan that both replenishes and protects the environment while providing the natural resources necessary for your state's citizens.
- Debate whether change is good. What makes it a good thing? When is it not good? How can we tell the difference?
- Have each student identify a time in his or her life when something changed; have students share their reactions to that change as they remember it.
- Build a consensus on the agreed-upon elements of your classroom time traveler museum.
- Identify the rules of conduct for visitors to a time traveler museum.
- Have students identify and share an important change they hope to contribute to society in their lifetime.
- Have each student perform a self-assessment on his or her work in this unit.

Learning Through Categories, Hierarchies, and Webbing

- Design a system for classifying change as good or bad. Test each proposed system and determine which systems work best.
- Categorize examples of change from American history as beneficial or counterproductive based on agreed-upon criteria.

- Create a hierarchical model of your state government and create a digital representation of the model.
- Build a database of endangered species in your state and post it on your class Web site.
- Identify the natural resources that need to be preserved in your state; devise a plan for saving them.
- Create a Venn diagram that shows flora and fauna indigenous to America and your state.
  - Have students rank significant historical events based on the effect they have on our lives today.
  - Organize the time traveler museum so that it is orderly and easy for people to walk through.
    - Categorize different jobs in the time traveler museum based on agreed-upon criteria.
    - Identify and classify each exhibit and piece in the time traveler museum for inclusion in an exhibit catalogue.

Learning Through Connections to Larger Understanding

- Construct models of how change operates, using different shapes that represent its continuous, altering nature.
- Create maps of students' lives showing the changes they've experienced in the past and events they anticipate in the future.
- Research each student's family history and publish student autobiographies.
- Study how families have changed in each century of American history. Focus on family size, roles, and configurations.
- Create a virtual tour of your town or state and post it online for visitors to share.
- Explore how the choices we make will determine the kinds of change people will experience in the future.
- Consider answers to the question "If change stops does growth stop?"
- Devise a philosophy of change that can be shared with others: What is change? What makes it helpful to humankind? How do we encourage positive change?
- Convert your classroom into a working time traveler museum that can be presented to visitors.
- Conduct tours through your museum that allow others to experience your understandings of change over time.

▶ Culminating Event:

Transform the classroom into a time traveler museum. Bring together all of the different understandings and work products students have constructed to celebrate in the museum exhibits. Have students take on roles in the museum so that they can perform as experts on what they have learned.

Resources:

 Books

Primary

    Araminta's Paint Box by Karen Ackerman
    The Backwards Watch by Eric Houghton
    The Best Town in the World by Byrd Baylor
    The Christmas House by Ann Turner
    The Keeping Quilt by Patricia Polacco
    Letting Swift River Go by Jane Yolen
    The Relatives Came by Cynthia Rylant
    A River Ran Wild: An Environmental History by Lynne Cherry
    Science Toolbox by Jean Stangl
    Town Mouse, Country Mouse by Jan Brett
    Tuesday by David Wiesner

Elementary

    Court of the Stone Children by Eleanor Cameron
    The Devil's Arithmetic by Jane Yolen
    Fog Magic by Julia Sauer
    A Girl Called Boy by Belinda Hurmence
    The House with a Clock in Its Walls by John Bellairs
    Jeremy Visick by David Wiseman
    Moon and I by Betsy Byars
    The Root Cellar by Janet Lunn
    Through the Lock by Carol Otis Hurst
    When I Was Young in the Mountains by Cynthia Rylant
    A Witch Across Time by Gilbert Cross

Middle School

    Across Five Aprils by Irene Hunt
    Adventures of Huckleberry Finn by Mark Twain
    Catherine, Called Birdie, The Midwife's Apprentice by Karen Cushman
    DK History of the World by Plantagenet Somerset Fry and Plantagenet S. Fry
    A Gathering of Days: A New England Girl's Journal by Joan Blos
    In the Year of the Boar and Jackie Robinson by Betty Bao Lord
    Jacob Have I Loved by Katherine Paterson
    Journey to Topaz by Yoshiko Uchida
    Summer of My German Soldier by Bette Greene
    The Watsons Go to Birmingham by Christopher Paul Curtis
    Witch of Balckbird Pond by Elizabeth George Speare

High School

    Babbit by Sinclair Lewis
    Daisy Miller by Henry James
    Gone with the Wind by Margaret Mitchell
    Hanta Yo: An American Saga by Ruth B. Hill

Native Son by Richard Wright
The Ox-Bow Incident by Walter Van Tilburg Clark
The Red Badge of Courage by Stephen Crane
Remembrance Rock by Carl Sandburg
The Scarlet Letter by Nathaniel Hawthorne
The Timetables of History: A Horizontal Linkage of People and Events by
Bernard Grun and Daniel J. Boorstin
To Kill a Mockingbird by Harper Lee

Music

Against the Wind—Bob Seeger
Album: Against the Wind

Big Yellow Taxi—Joni Mitchell
Album: Ladies of the Canyon

The Boy in the Bubble—Paul Simon
Album: Graceland

A Change is Gonna Come—The Band
Album: Moondog Matinee

My City was Gone—The Pretenders
Album: Learning to Crawl

New Year's Day—U2
Album: War

Reeling in the Years—Steely Dan
Album: Greatest Hits

Time Passages—Al Stewart
Album: Time Passages

The Times They are a Changin'—Bob Dylan
Album: The Times They are a Changin'

Turn! Turn! Turn!—The Byrds
Album: Turn! Turn! Turn!

@ Web Resources

Age of Protest and Change
<http://www.byu.edu/ipt/projects/1960s/>

American Experience
<http://www.pbs.org/wgbh/amex/archives.html>

American Immigration
<http://www.bergen.org/AAST/Projects/Immigration/index.html>

American Memory
<http://lcweb2.loc.gov/ammem/amhome.html>

American West
<http://www.americanwest.com/>

Archiving Early America
<http://earlyamerica.com/>

The Costume Page
<http://users.aol.com/nebula5/tcpinfo2.html>

Exploratorium Online Activities
<http://www.exploratorium.edu/explore/online.html>

Eyewitness
<http://www.ibiscom.com/index.html>

Flags of the World
<http://www.fotw.ca/flags/>

Global Grocery List Project
<http://www.landmark-project.com/ggl/>

Great Buildings Collection
<http://www.greatbuildings.com/gbc.html>

History of Toys and Games
<http://www.historychannel.com/cgi-bin/frameit.cgi?p=http%3A//www.historychannel.com/exhibits/toys/bears.html>

HyperHistory
<http://www.hyperhistory.com/online_n2/History_n2/a.html>

Kids' Castle
<http://www.kidscastle.si.edu/>

Native Pre-Contact Housing
<http://www.kstrom.net/isk/maps/houses/housingmap.html>

NativeWeb
<http://www.nativeweb.org/>

The Old Timer's Page
<http://waltonfeed.com/old/index.html>

Oral History Online
<http://bancroft.berkeley.edu/ROHO/ohonline/>

PBS History
<http://www.pbs.org/neighborhoods/history/>

Playing with Time
<http://www.playingwithtime.org/>

Radio Days
<http://www.otr.com/index.shtml>

United States Historical Census Data Browser
<http://fisher.lib.virginia.edu/census/>

Voting and Registration Data
<http://www.census.gov/population/www/socdemo/voting.html>

You Be the Historian
<http://americanhistory.si.edu/hohr/springer/>

Featured Software Title

Timeliner

<http://www.tomsnyder.com/classroom/timelineronline/?ref=timeliner.com>

Timeliner allows students to create their own timelines in one of several formats, including a multimedia timeline that incorporates digital sound and video, and can be shown as a slideshow. Timeliner is an indispensable tool in the classroom.

✚ Building Understanding:

1. How can the concept of changes be examined in other disciplines, aside from the study of history?

2. How can the Changes unit be adapted to accommodate varying grade levels?

3. How will you have students self-assess their work in this unit?

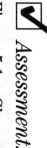

Assessment:

Figure 5.1—Changes Unit Participation Rubric

Participation	Needs Improvement 1	Satisfactory 2	Exemplary 3
Participates in class activities.	Occasionally when interested in the task.	Regularly whenever prompted to join.	Consistently with interest and enthusiasm.
Cooperates with peers.	Depends on whom he or she is working with.	Shares and works cooperatively.	Serves as a role model for sharing and cooperating.
Is a collaborative partner.	Does not share ideas or does not listen to others.	Collaborates to successfully complete tasks.	Is a class leader in forming collaborative partnerships.
Demonstrates an understanding of the dynamic of change.	Does not demonstrate an understanding that change is necessary for growth and change.	Demonstrates a working understanding of how change is necessary for growth and progress.	Demonstrates a working understanding of how change is necessary for growth and progress, which the learner then applies to new and different situations.
Demonstrated mastery of skills specified in state standards.	Did not meet the minimum requirements for state standards targeted in this unit.	Met the minimum requirements for state standards targeted in this unit.	Exceeded the minimum requirements for state standards targeted in this unit.

Figure 5.2—Changes Unit Project Rubric

Project	Needs Improvement 1	Satisfactory 2	Exemplary 3
Is done neatly with attention to detail.	Project is incomplete or lacks sufficient depth.	Project is neat and shows attention to detail.	Project is neat, shows attention to detail, and exhibits craftsmanship that goes beyond grade-level expectations
Is based in an identified content area of the unit.	Is not related to any content area being studied under the theme of change.	Is based in one identified content area.	Is based in two or more identified content areas.
Applies skills and concepts in a new or different way.	Project imitates objects or examples studied in class.	Project demonstrates mastery of skills and concepts in a unique way.	Project demonstrates mastery of skills and concepts in a unique way at the highest level of thinking.
Adds to the class study of change.	Does not add to the class experience or understanding of change.	Adds to the class understanding of change.	Adds to the class understanding of change by elevating the level of discussion or activity.
Demonstrated high personal standards for work.	Does not demonstrate high personal standards in the completion of the project.	Demonstrates high standards for work as outlined by the teacher and/or class.	Demonstrates high personal standards for work that exceeds teacher expectations.

Chapter 6

Celebrate the
Electoral Process

This Choices unit empowers students to take part in the electoral process right in your classroom. It's ideal for use in a national election year but can be utilized in any school year to help capture the excitement of the democratic process. The result is a classroom election and the use of the legislative process to facilitate student ownership in the classroom.

AGE: Middle School, but can be adapted to any grade level

Standards:

National English Language Arts Standards—
NCTE/IRA National Council of Teachers of English (2001).

1. Adjust use of spoken, written, and visual language (e.g., conventions, style, vocabulary) to communicate effectively with a variety of audiences and for different purposes.

2. Develop an understanding of and respect for diversity in language use, patterns, and dialects across cultures, ethnic groups, geographic regions, and social roles.

3. Use spoken, written, and visual language to accomplish their own purposes (e.g., for learning, enjoyment, persuasion, and the exchange of information).

Standards for the English Language Arts, by the International Reading Association and the National Council of Teachers of English, Copyright 1996 by the International Reading Association and the National Council of Teachers of English. Reprinted with permission.

National Mathematics Standards—
NCTM National Council of Teachers of Mathematics (2000).

1. Compute fluently and make reasonable estimate.
2. Use mathematical models to represent and understand quantitative relationships.
3. Formulate questions that can be addressed with data and collect, organize, and display relevant data to answer them.
4. Develop and evaluate inferences and predictions that are based on data.
5. Make and investigate mathematical conjectures.
6. Organize and consolidate mathematical thinking through communication.
7. Recognize and apply mathematics in contexts outside of mathematics.

Standards are listed with the permission of the National Council of Teachers of Mathematics (NCTM). NCTM does not endorse the content or validity of these alignments.

National Science Standards—
NAS National Academy of Science (1995).

1. Scientific explanations incorporate existing scientific knowledge and new evidence from observations, experiments, or models into internally consistent, logical statements.

Reprinted with permission from "What Is the Influence of the National Science Education Standards?: Reviewing the Evidence, A Workshop Summary" (2003) by the National Academy of Sciences, courtesy of the National Academies Press, Washington, D.C.

National Social Studies Standards—NCSS
National Council for the Social Studies (1997).

1. Institutions such as schools, churches, families, government agencies, and the courts all play an integral role in our lives.
2. An understanding of civic ideals and practices of citizenship is critical to full participation in society and is a central purpose of the social studies.

Permission to reprint standards granted by the National Council of Social Studies Publications.

THEME: *Choices*

! **Big Idea:** Your choices determine your options.

? **Need to Know Questions:**

1. Do you have to choose?
2. How do you know all your choices?
3. What makes a bad choice?
4. What makes one choice better than others?

★ **Mission:**

Give your students the following instructions and allow them to discuss which choice they would like to make as a group:

> "Good news! I have decided that we need some leadership to help move things along in our classroom. We can either allow me (the teacher) to appoint someone to be that leader for the group, or we can allow the class to determine who the leader will be. Now, there are implications for whatever choice you make. If you allow me to choose a leader, then you must trust my judgment and you must understand that there will be no discussion about my choice. Furthermore, you will be expected to follow the class leader I appoint in whatever direction he or she wishes to lead you. You also cannot question the style of the leader I appoint. You must simply accept whomever I select.
>
> Your other choice is to have the class select a leader. This is not a responsibility to be taken lightly. It will take time to determine who will be considered. It will also require effort on your part to give all persons nominated a fair consideration based on their ideas and abilities. Once time has been provided for each candidate to be considered, the students will then have to vote for the person they would most like to lead.
>
> This is an important choice, one that will affect the rest of your school year. So let's discuss which choice you will make as a group. Be ready to explain the reasons for your ideas and to question your classmates' ideas, as well."

Allow time for students to discuss which option they would like to choose. Help them to explore the electoral process, and the procedures for fairly nominating candidates, campaigning, and voting. Make sure they understand that you are talking days and weeks, not minutes and hours. Help them to make a choice in which they can find a consensus of agreement.

Learning Tasks:

 ## Learning Through Language

- Research the electoral process on the state and federals. Point out important points about the structure of American elections.
- Interview a member of local government about the electoral process. Follow up with a summary of what the class has learned from the exchange.
- Conduct a weekly round table forum in which all students will speak on behalf of their own ideas. Select a timely topic each week on which students will focus the discussion.
- Allow time for your class to iron out the procedures and issues related to your classroom electoral process. Agree to set practices that everyone will abide by throughout the unit.
- Have each candidate give a campaign speech. Follow the speech with a question and answer session in which classmates may probe deeper for insight into each candidate's ideas.
- Conduct a campaign rally for each candidate in which all class members participate. Provide campaign buttons, signs, and banners for each candidate.
- Write a platform of ideas and goals for each candidate. Assign specific issues that the class has agreed upon. Have the class vote on each platform and then split into two political parties.
- Conduct a press conference in which students may question each candidate. Have students each write an article summing up their perception of the press conference.
- Write campaign slogans and campaign literature for each candidate. Have students publish their literature and print it out for distribution.
- Write letters in support of candidates. Publish them in a classroom newspaper editorial page.

 ## Learning Through Problem Solving

- Create a visual map of the process for making a good choice. Agree on one map that will be posted in the classroom.
- Identify a bad choice made in a piece of children's literature. Select a better choice for the character and web how that decision would change the circumstances for the character in question.
- Identify issues that need to be addressed by a class leader. Accept all ideas and then narrow the list to the top five issues a classroom leader can realistically address.
- Chart the step-by-step process for nominating, campaigning, and voting for candidates. Look for gaps in the chart and revise it until everyone agrees that it is thorough and complete.
- Research how a bill becomes a law at the state and federal levels. Have students create their own semantic maps that delineate this process.

- Study the electoral college system and determine how many votes your state has in the electoral college. Research how many times your state has voted for the winning candidate in the electoral college over the history of U.S. presidential elections.
- Create measurement guidelines for political campaign posters, buttons, and leaflets. Require students to work within those guidelines as they create campaign literature for their candidate.
- Agree upon voting booth design and dimensions. Make sure students take into consideration ergonomic factors for all students in your classroom.
- Devise a process for counting ballots for your classroom election. Include a way to verify vote counts and break a tie vote.
- Based on evidence gathered from class discussions, predict the outcome of your class vote on specific issues.

Learning Through Seeing and Imagining

- Study the symbols of the major American political parties. Create a catalogue of political symbols.
- Create political symbols to represent each political party in your classroom, based on student research of political symbols.
- Design campaign posters for each candidate that incorporate elements of American political symbolism.
- Construct campaign buttons for each candidate that use symbolism consistent with classroom party emblems and campaign posters.
- Use a desktop publishing program to publish flyers or leaflets that promote each candidate.
- Organize the classroom so that each candidate has his or her own campaign headquarters. Hang party banners to mark the area for each campaign.
- Have each candidate agree on a specific color or colors to be worn by supporters of each candidate on campaign and voting days.
- Study political cartoon archives online that cover the history of American politics. Emphasize cartoons that focus on issues rather than candidates.
- Draw original political cartoons which target a specific classroom issue that should be addressed.
- Present a student-designed PowerPoint presentation on each candidate prior to class voting. Include digital photographs, political symbols, and campaign slogans in the presentations.

Learning Through Patterns

- Listen to songs about choices. Discuss the choice being made in each song and the issues that come into play in making good choices.

- Identify recurring choices students have in the classroom. Come up with a pattern students can recognize for making good choices.
- Examine choices Americans make on a regular basis. Compare these choices and their patterns with the choices students make in the classroom.
- Listen to political campaign jingles from past elections. Discuss how different jingles reflect the issues and attitudes of their times.
- Create original campaign jingles for your classroom candidates, which can be sung at campaign rallies and speeches.
- Agree on graphic design patterns that can be used by a candidate in all posters, buttons, and literature.
- Create original chants and cheers that supporters of each candidate can use for speeches and rallies.
- Study voting patterns from a past local, state, or national election.
- Study voting patterns by gender and identify the major issues that men and women value in making election choices.
- Project voting patterns for future state elections based on your findings.

❀ Learning Through Interaction with the Environment

- Act out skits that demonstrate good and bad choices. They may be based on children's literature or generated from original student ideas.
- Play games and simulations that allow students to see how choices affect the outcome of a situation.
- Construct campaign buttons using available classroom materials.
- Build voting booths based on student specifications.
- At campaign rallies, spell out each candidate's name using your body to form each letter.
- Devise campaign handshakes for each candidate.
- Make and wear campaign hats in support of candidates.
- Sponsor a parade in support of each candidate.
- Count ballots manually and verify vote counts.
- Have an inauguration ceremony for the elected candidate.

🤝 Learning Through Interaction with Others

- Reflect on how our choices affect others. Discuss how we feel when we are affected by a good or bad choice.
- Research important choices made in our history and how the town, state, or nation came to agree on the best choice.

- Study what happens when we cannot agree on a choice. Discuss the concept of compromise.
- Practice the skill of building a consensus on class issues. Model how to negotiate with stakeholders to bring everyone into agreement.
- Invite supporters of each candidate to form a campaign committee.
- Work in groups to plan campaign rallies.
- Present persuasive speeches on behalf of an issue or a candidate.
- Participate in class debates.
- Invite those candidates not elected to join the cabinet of the elected leader to help work on classroom issues together.
- Craft classroom legislation and vote to pass or defeat it.

♥ Learning Through Feelings, Values, and Attitudes

- Agree on criteria for determining what makes a choice good or bad.
- Differentiate between an individual's goals and the goals of the greater good.
- Explore how a person's value system helps him or her to make choices.
- Discuss issues in a way that allows each student to have his or her point of view.
- View choices in light of a larger goal students want to achieve.
- Consider how your choices can help or hinder your goals.
- Practice making choices using creative problem-solving techniques: identify a problem, agree on criteria for solving the problem, brainstorm solutions, rank the solutions by rating them against the agreed-upon criteria.
- Study the values of the major political parties.
- Study the values of each classroom party. Do they parallel national parties?
- Use a Web site and database to have students electronically vote for a candidate to be class leader.

▣ Learning Through Categories, Hierarchies, and Webbing

- Sort American presidents by agreed-upon class criteria.
- Categorize classroom issues by agreed-upon criteria.
- Classify each candidate by his or her stand on classroom issues.
- Survey voters and categorize the issues that are important to them from most important to least important.
- Enter data from the surveys into a spreadsheet and create graphs that visually represent the data.
- Build a database of survey data that allows students to examine issues from different demographics (age, gender, supporter of which candidate).
- Study the categories of state or national liberal, moderate, and conservative voters.
- Analyze state or national voting results based on demographic data.
- Study the branches of your state and federal governments based on the checks and balances of power.
- Create a hierarchical model of your classroom government.

Learning Through Connections to Larger Understanding

- Explore why government is necessary.
- Compare a classroom with a student government with a classroom without student representation.
- Understand a philosophy of democratic government. Compare it with other forms of government currently in existence.
- Discuss ethical behavior in campaigning.
- Create a Web site for each classroom candidate that espouses the class' platform and welcomes voter support.
- Examine classroom issues from the perspective of each candidate.
- Critique election paraphernalia from past campaigns based on visual attractiveness.
- Summarize the election results in terms of which issues carried the election.
- Create a classroom government.
- Build a classroom community based on the classroom government.

 Culminating Event:

Conduct a classroom election and build a student government based upon the results. Have an inauguration ceremony and invite all members of the class to participate actively in their government.

 Resources:

📖 Books

Primary

    Anansi Finds a Fool by Verna Aardema
    And so they Build by Burt Kitchen
    Charlie Needs a Cloak by Tomie de Paola
    The Doorbell Rang by Pat Hutchins
    Frederick by Leo Lionni
    If You Give a Mouse a Cookie by Laura J. Numeroff
    Jake Johnson: The Story of a Mule by Tres Seymour
    Sylvester and the Magic Pebble by William Steig
    The Tale of Peter Rabbit by Beatrix Potter
    Treeful of Pigs by Arnold Lobel
    Who Sank the Boat? By Pamela Allen

Elementary

    Annie and the Old One by Miska Miles
    Arnold Ballot Box Battle by Emily McCully

Baseball Saved Us by Ken Mochizuki
Class President by Johanna Hurwitz
Frindle by Andrew Clements
The Great Turkey Walk by Kathleen Karr
Midnight Fox by Betsy Byars
Sarah, Plain and Tall by Patricia MacLachlan
Traitor: the Case of Benedict Arnold by Jean Fritz
Weasel by Cynthia DeFelice
You Want Women to Vote, Lizzie Stanton? by Jean Fritz

Middle School

A Connecticut Yankee in King Arthur's Court by Mark Twain
Building Blocks by Cynthia Voigt
December Stillness by Mary Downing Hahn
The Devil's Arithmetic by Jane Yolen
From the Mixed-Up Files of Mrs. Basil E. Frankweiler by E.L. Konigsburg
Landslide!: A Kid's Guide to the U.S. Elections by Dan Gutman
Over Sea, Under Stone by Susan Cooper
Parrot in the Oven: Mi Vida by Victor Martinez
Voices After Midnight by Richard Peck
Whipping Boy by Sid Fleischman
A Wrinkle in Time by Madeleine L'Engle

High School

Around the World in Eighty Days by Jules Verne
Brave New World by Aldous Huxley
Gulliver's Travels by Jonathan Swift
*How To Win a High School Election: Advice and Ideas from Over 1,000
    High School Seniors* by Jeff Marx
Les Miserables by Victor Hugo
Looking Backward: 2000–1887 by Edward Bellamy
Nineteen Eighty-Four by George Orwell
Slaughterhouse-Five by Kurt Vonnegut
Time and Again by Jack Finney
The Time Machine by H.G. Wells
Wuthering Heights by Emily Bronte

Music

American Tune—Paul Simon
Album: There Goes Rhymin' Simon

Doctor My Eyes—Jackson Browne
Album: Jackson Browne

Don't Dream It's Over—Crowded House
Album: Crowded House

Don't Stop—Fleetwood Mac
Album: Rumours

Everybody Wants to Rule the World—Tears for Fears
Album: Songs from the Big Chair

Future's So Bright I Gotta Wear Shades—Timbuk3
Album: Greetings from Timbuk3

Learning to Fly—Tom Petty
Album: Into the Great Wide Open

Right Now—Van Halen
Album: For Unlawful Carnal Knowledge

Things Can Only Get Better—Howard Jones
Album: Dream into Action

We've Only Just Begun—The Carpenters
Album: The Singles (1969–1973)

 Web Resources

Alexa Web Search
<http://download.alexa.com/alexa65/startpage.html?p=Dest_W_t_40_B1>

Avalon Project
<http://www.yale.edu/lawweb/avalon/avalon.htm>

Ben's Guide to Government for Kids
<http://bensguide.gpo.gov/>

Brain Warp
<http://www.spaceday.com/en/mission/brainwarp/index.php>

Can Do!
<http://www.ucando.org/>

Cast Your Vote!
<http://www.learner.org/exhibits/statistics/>

Don't Buy It
<http://pbskids.org/dontbuyit/>

Dumb Laws
<http://www.dumblaws.com/>

Electoral College Calculator
<http://www.julienne.com/weblog.html>

End Game
<http://www.pbs.org/endgame/home.php>

Escape from Knab
<http://www.escapefromknab.com/>

Every Four Years
<http://www.newseum.org/everyfouryears/>

Inside Art
<http://www.eduweb.com/insideart/>

Iz and Auggie Go to the Polls
<http://www.headbone.com/derby/polls/>

Jo Fool or Jo Cool
<http://www.media-awareness.ca/english/special_initiatives/games/joecool_joefool/jo_cool_kids.cfm>

Kids Democracy Project
<http://www.pbs.org/democracy/kids/>

Kids Voting USA
<http://www.kidsvotingusa.org/>

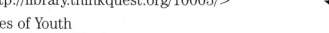

Learning Adventures in Citizenship
<http://www.pbs.org/wnet/newyork/laic/index.html>

Making Good Choices for Life
<http://library.thinkquest.org/J001709/>

Peace Corps Kids World
<http://www.peacecorps.gov/kids/>

Polling Report
<http://www.pollingreport.com/>

The 30 Second Candidate
<http://www.pbs.org/30secondcandidate/>

Unica Island
<http://library.thinkquest.org/10005/>

Voices of Youth
<http://www.unicef.org/voy/>

The White House Project
<http://www.thewhitehouseproject.org/>

Featured Software Title

Print Shop Deluxe

<http://www.broderbund.com/Product.asp?OID=4152050>
Print Shop Deluxe brings all kinds of graphic images and desktop publishing power to your computers. Students can use this productivity suite to create all kinds of banners, posters, brochures, certificates, and buttons as part of your comprehensive classroom technology integration plan.

Building Understanding:

1. How can a study of choices help address student choices in behavior?

2. How can implementing this unit during a state or national election year provide an additional dimension to the student learning experience?

3. What will you use for student work products in this election unit?

Assessment:

Figure 6.1—Choices Unit Participation Rubric

Participation	Needs Improvement 1	Satisfactory 2	Exemplary 3
Participates in class activities.	Occasionally when interested in the task.	Regularly whenever prompted to join.	Consistently with interest and enthusiasm.
Cooperates with peers.	Depends on whom he or she is working with.	Shares and works cooperatively.	Serves as a role model for sharing and cooperating.
Is a collaborative partner.	Does not share ideas or does not listen to others.	Collaborates to successfully complete tasks.	Is a class leader in forming collaborative partnerships.
Demonstrates an understanding of the implications of choice.	Does not demonstrate an understanding that choices have implications.	Demonstrates a working understanding of how choices have implications.	Demonstrates a working understanding of how choices have implications which the learner then applies to new and different choices.
Demonstrated mastery of skills specified in state standards.	Did not meet the minimum requirements for state standards targeted in this unit.	Met the minimum requirements for state standards targeted in this unit.	Exceeded the minimum requirements for state standards targeted in this unit.

Figure 6.2—Choices Unit Project Rubric

Project	Needs Improvement 1	Satisfactory 2	Exemplary 3
Is done neatly with attention to detail.	Project is incomplete or lacks sufficient depth.	Project is neat and shows attention to detail.	Project is neat, shows attention to detail, and exhibits craftsmanship that goes beyond grade-level expectations
Is based in an identified content area of the unit.	Is not related to any content area.	Is based in one identified content area.	Is based in two or more identified content areas.
Applies skills and concepts in a new or different way.	Project imitates objects or examples studied in class.	Project demonstrates mastery of skills and concepts in a unique way.	Project demonstrates mastery of skills and concepts in a unique way at the highest level of thinking.
Adds to the class study of choices.	Does not add to the class experience or understanding of choices.	Adds to the class understanding of choices.	Adds to the class understanding of choices by elevating the level of discussion or activity.
Demonstrated high personal standards for work.	Does not demonstrate high personal standards in the completion of the project.	Demonstrates high standards for work as outlined by the teacher and/or class.	Demonstrates high personal standards for work that exceeds teacher expectations.

Chapter 7

Select a Blue Ribbon Example of Architecture

T his Construction unit entrusts students with the job of surveying your community's architecture and developing a system wherein the most exemplary building will be recognized in your hometown. This is an especially invigorating unit for visual learners.

AGE: Elementary School, but can be adapted to any grade level

Standards:

National English Language Arts Standards—
NCTE/IRA National Council of Teachers of English (2001).

1. Conduct research on issues and interests by generating ideas and questions, and by posing problems. Gather, evaluate, and synthesize data from a variety of sources (e.g., print and non-print texts, artifacts, people) to communicate their discoveries in ways that suit their purpose and audience.

2. Use a variety of technological and information resources (e.g., libraries, databases, computer networks, video) to gather and synthesize information and to create and communicate knowledge.

3. Participate as knowledgeable, reflective, creative, and critical members of a variety of literacy communities.

Standards for the English Language Arts, by the International Reading Association and the National Council of Teachers of English, Copyright 1996 by the International Reading Association and the National Council of Teachers of English. Reprinted with permission.

National Mathematics Standards—
NCTM National Council of Teachers of Mathematics (2000).

1. Analyze characteristics and properties of two- and 3-D geometric shapes and develop mathematical arguments about geometric relationships.
2. Apply transformations and use symmetry to analyze mathematical situations.
3. Use visualization, spatial reasoning, and geometric modeling to solve problems.
4. Apply appropriate techniques, tools, and formulas to determine measurements.
5. Apply and adapt a variety of appropriate strategies to solve problems.
6. Communicate their mathematical thinking coherently and clearly to peers, teachers, and others.

Standards are listed with the permission of the National Council of Teachers of Mathematics (NCTM). NCTM does not endorse the content or validity of these alignments.

National Science Standards—
NAS National Academy of Science (1995).

1. Form and function are complementary aspects of objects, organisms, and systems in the natural and designed world.

Reprinted with permission from "What Is the Influence of the National Science Education Standards?: Reviewing the Evidence, A Workshop Summary" (2003) by the National Academy of Sciences, courtesy of the National Academies Press, Washington, D.C.

National Social Studies Standards—
NCSS National Council for the Social Studies (1997).

1. Human beings create, learn, and adapt culture.
2. Human beings seek to understand their historical roots and to locate themselves in time.
3. The study of people, places, and human-environment interactions assists learners as they create their spatial views and geographic perspectives of the world.

Permission to reprint standards granted by the National Council of Social Studies Publications.

THEME: *Construction*

 Big Idea: People build products, ideas, and relationships.

 Need to Know Questions:

1. Why do people build?
2. In what ways do we build?
3. What do we use to build?
4. What are the steps in building?
5. Can we build too much?

 Mission:

Read to the class the following charge:

> "Congratulations! You have been selected to form a blue ribbon committee that studies the architecture of your hometown and identifies one building that best exemplifies your town's history, values, and customs! To accomplish this, you will need to:
>
> 1. Identify elements in architecture that successfully reflect your town's history, values, and customs.
> 2. Collect images of architecture in your community.
> 3. Rank the structures from the best to the least, using the elements you have identified.
> 4. Select the one building that is to receive the blue ribbon award as the best example of your community's architecture."

Allow time for students to discuss what kinds of history, values, and customs their town celebrates, how they will gather images, and how they will judge each image to find the best example of local architecture. Once all ideas have been discussed, begin planning a timeline of when each step will be accomplished.

 Learning Tasks:

 Learning Through Language

- Agree on ground rules for working as a blue ribbon committee.
- Read information books on architecture through the ages.
- Brainstorm all ideas on your town's history, values, and customs. Accept all answers.
- Discuss which characteristics of your town are most likely to be seen in its architecture.
- Agree on a list of elements to look for in each image you collect.

- Research elements of architecture through the ages. Identify eastern, western, classical, medieval, colonial, and modern periods and styles.
- Report to the class an architectural styles including Greek, Roman, Renaissance, Gothic, Georgian, Federal, and any other styles that may be evidenced in your region.
- Have an architect speak to the class about the skills needed to design structures.
- Discuss each image by identifying its architectural elements and coming to a consensus on how it should be ranked.
- As each structure is reviewed, have students right a summary of its architectural elements and style, including a reference to community history, values, or customs.
- Create a digital catalogue that includes each structure reviewed by your class and the summary of architectural elements captioned below each image.
- Write to the local newspaper and announce your class's choice of the best example of local architecture.

💡 Learning Through Problem Solving

- Study the physics of architecture. Explore what is structurally sound and what principles are used to make a structure stronger.
- Estimate structure size and mass based on visual observation.
- Practice measuring structures by size and mass using appropriate tools for measurement.
- Convert measurements to metric standards.
- Use formulas to determine the strength of a structure by measuring the stress on important joints.
- Study the laws of physics that are used in demolishing a structure.
- Research local laws on zoning and building in your community.
- Propose solutions for existing structural problems in local architecture. Compare suggested solutions with existing building codes to verify that they are plausible.
- Research the costs associated with creating each piece of architecture reviewed.
- Predict which buildings will be the best examples of local architecture.
- Identify the best example of local architecture using identified criteria.

👁 Learning Through Seeing and Imagining

- Web all the different kinds of architectural elements to look for in your community.
- Take digital pictures of each example of architecture to be considered.
- Use a graphics editor to import each digital image and highlight architectural elements to be considered by the class.
- Use the graphics editor to flip, rotate, and mirror structures and individual architectural elements.

- Practice drawing and reading blueprints.
- Use a desktop publishing application to create sketches that illustrate the physical design of each structure.
- Design a sequence of diagrams that visually shows each step of the construction process.
- Build a slideshow that presents each building considered with a caption stating its identified architectural elements and the ways in which it exemplifies local history, values, and customs.

- Create a picture book that shows the sequential process of building the structure your class has selected as the best example of local architecture, in the style of David MacAulay.
- Publish the building that has been selected as the best example of local architecture on your school Web site.

Learning Through Patterns

- Find patterns in local architecture.
- Identify unique attributes of local architecture.
- Read and recite poetry about building products, ideas, and relationships.
- Write concrete poems that describe each building your class studies.
- Listen to songs about building products, ideas, and relationships. Study the lyrics of the songs for important themes and ideas.
- Listen to music from ancient Greece, Rome, the Renaissance, and other cultures and eras that are reflected in local architecture.
- Study the design and structure of musical instruments. Identify common principles found between the construction of musical instruments and local architecture.
- Identify similarities and differences between classic architecture and modern architecture.
- Apply architectural patterns in prototypes of buildings that may be built in the future.
- Add music to an architecture slideshow that reflects the spirit of the architecture in your community.

Learning Through Interaction with the Environment

- Take a walking tour of your community. Have students take pictures of buildings they would like to be considered by the blue ribbon committee.
- Visit a construction site and identify the materials and methods being used to build the structure.
- Use visual art materials to create reproductions of local buildings with interesting architectural elements.
- Form examples of architectural elements using clay.
- Use tools and wood to practice building joints and joists.
- Build bridges out of craft sticks. Allow students to use different designs to ensure strength. Test each bridge by rolling a 10-pound truck across it.

- Construct skyscrapers out of plastic straws. Allow students to create original designs that allow them to build tall and sturdy structures. The building that is the tallest and stands free is recognized as being the best design.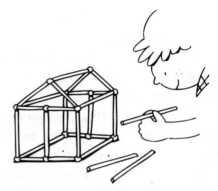
- Create an original building design using available materials (cardboard, wood, paper) that can be displayed on a desktop or flat surface. Allow students to incorporate architectural elements of their choosing that reflect their history, values, and customs.
- Build a classroom-sized model of the building that best represents local architecture. Use available materials to form the façade. Color the building accurately.
- Design and place a blue ribbon on the finished model.

Learning Through Interaction with Others

- Work as a blue ribbon committee in a constructive, supportive way.
- Build a consensus on the architectural elements that are significant in your community.
- Form subcommittees to study each building considered.
- Talk with architects, contractors, and local government officials to learn more about the construction process.
- Share ideas, abilities, and materials, as class members work together.
- Correspond with classes willing to share their local architecture, history, values, and customs.
- Make a persuasive case for the best example of local architecture.
- Share your class's findings with the owners and occupants of the building you have selected as the best example of local architecture.
- Invite other classes and the local community to visit your display of the best example of local architecture.
- Receive input from community members who wish to comment on your class's selection.

Learning Through Feelings, Values, and Attitudes

- Study Frank Lloyd Wright's work and appreciate his values for architectural design.
- Explore the ways local architecture complements or clashes with the environment.
- Identify your community's values, traditions, and heritage.
- Study your community's history and famous citizens.
- Share what students like best about your community.
- Distinguish the social values that are reflected in your local architecture.
- Assign a value expressed by each architectural element studied (for example, a dome may be assigned the value of continuity and repetition).

- Consider the importance of line, form, symmetry, balance, and color in architecture. How does each of these things affect your feeling about a structure?
- Establish criteria for each architectural element. How will you determine if it is being used successfully? How will you measure that success?
- Use a rubric to evaluate each building.

Learning Through Categories, Hierarchies, and Webbing

- Build a database of information on each building your class studies.
- Sort local architecture by agreed-upon attributes.
- Categorize local architecture by agreed-upon criteria.
- Design a timeline of local architecture.
- Create new architectural elements and trace their forms back to existing architectural elements and traditions.
- Construct a rubric that will measure the success of each building in terms of architectural elements.
- Rank local architecture based on each student's personal taste.
- Rank local architecture using your rubric. How do the rankings differ from personal tastes?
- Create a hierarchy of local architecture based upon rubric rankings.
- Organize your images of local architecture into a sequential slideshow, culminating in your class' choice for the single best example of local architecture.
- Identify classical and modern elements of architecture found in your blue ribbon selection.

Learning Through Connections to Larger Understanding

- Compare the building of structures with the building of ideas and relationships. How are they the same?
- Understand the inspection process for building safe, secure structures.
- Consider how construction can help or hurt a community.
- Explore how architecture reflects a community's values.
- Study your community's neighborhoods and districts.
- Embrace a specific philosophy of architecture that will help your class in identifying its blue ribbon selection.
- Summarize how all the architectural elements in your blue ribbon selection come together to successfully reflect your community's history, values, and customs.
- Collect images that show many different perspectives of your blue ribbon selection.
- Critique your blue ribbon selection using art and architectural terms that describe its structural and artistic integrity.
- Describe a future architectural vision for your community that will respect your local history while helping your community grow and evolve. What will the downtown area look like? Why?

Culminating Event:

Invite local dignitaries and media to cover the announcement of your selection of the best example of local architecture. Showcase your classroom-sized model of the building and invite feedback from visitors on your selection.

 Resources:

 Books

Primary

Building by Elisha Cooper
The Butterfly House by Eve Bunting
Circles, Triangles, and Squares by Tana Hoban
Look-Alikes: Discover a Land Where Things Are Not as They Appear... by Joan Steiner
Moondogs by Kirk Daniel
The Secret Birthday Message by Eric Carle
Sector 7 by David Wiesner
Truck by Donald Crews
The Very Busy Spider by Eric Carle
Workshop by Andrew Clements

Elementary

Ancient Cliff Dwellers of Mesa Verde by Caroline Arnold
Boy of the Three-Year Nap by Dianne Snyder
Bringing the Rain to Kapiti Plain by Verna Aardema
Castle by David Macaulay
Dragonwings by Laurence Yep
Little House on the Prairie by Laura Ingalls Wilder
Nana Upstairs and Nana Downstairs by Tomie dePaola
New Way Things Work by David Macaulay
Seedfolks by Paul Fleischman
Ten Mile Day and the Building of the Transcontinental Railroad by Mary Ann Fraser

Middle School

Bridge to Terabithia by Katherine Paterson
Dragon's Gate by Laurence Yep
Forty Acres and Maybe a Mule by Harriette Gillem Robinet
The Great Fire by Jim Murphy
    Maya Lin by Bettina Ling
My Side of the Mountain by Jean Craighead George
Our House: The Stories of Levittown by Pamela Conrad
Slake's Limbo by Felice Holman
Time Apart, A by Diane Stanley
Unbuilding by David Macaulay (see also City and Cathedral)

High School

> *Animal Farm* by George Orwell
> *Architecture: Form, Space, and Order* by Frank D.K. Ching
> *Doctor Zhivago* by Boris Paternak
> *Frankenstein* by Mary Shelley
> *Heart of Darkness* by Joseph Conrad
> *Lord of the Flies* by William Golding
> *Main Street* by Sinclair Lewis
> *My Antonia* by Willa Cather
> *Robinson Crusoe* by Daniel DeFoe
> *Things Fall Apart* by Chinua Achebe
> *The Tin Drum* by Gunter Grass

 # Music

Allentown—Billy Joel
Album: Nylon Curtain

America—Neil Diamond
Album: The Jazz Singer

Back on the Chain Gang—The Pretenders
Album: Learning to Crawl

Bridge Over Troubled Water—Simon and Garfunkel
Album: Bridge Over Troubled Water

Building the Perfect Beast—Don Henley
Album: Building the Perfect Beast

City of New Orleans—Arlo Guthrie
Album: The Best of Arlo Guthrie

Fixing a Hole—The Beatles
Album: Sgt. Pepper's Lonely Hearts Club Band

If I Had a Hammer—Peter, Paul and Mary
Album: Ten Years Together

Under the Bridge—Red Hot Chili Peppers
Album: What Hits!?

Up On the Roof—James Taylor
Album: Flag

 # Web Resources

Architecture for Kids
<http://www.takus.com/architecture/>

Architecture of Thomas Jefferson
<http://www.bc.edu/bc_org/avp/cas/fnart/fa267/Jeffersn.html>

Archkidecture
<http://www.archkidecture.org/>

Art & Architecture
<http://www.arlington.k12.va.us/schools/drew/a&a/a&a.htm>

Art & Architecture Thesaurus
<http://www.getty.edu/research/tools/vocabulary/aat/>

Building Big
<http://www.pbs.org/wgbh/buildingbig/>

Building the Chrysler Building
<http://xroads.virginia.edu/~1930s/DISPLAY/chrysler/front.html>

Building Stuff
<http://www.dot.state.tx.us/kidsonly/buildstuff/Buildstuff.html>

Building Surprises
<http://hudson.acad.umn.edu/surprises/index.html>

The Construction of the Empire State Building, 1930–1931
<http://www.nypl.org/research/chss/spe/art/photo/hinex/empire/empire.html>

Decopix
<http://www.decopix.com/>

Digital Archive of Architecture
<http://www.bc.edu/bc_org/avp/cas/fnart/arch/default.html>

Federal Style Architecture
<http://jan.ucc.nau.edu/~twp/architecture/federal/>

Frederick Law Olmstead
<http://fredericklawolmsted.com/>

Georgian Colonial Architecture
<http://www.salemweb.com/guide/arch/georgian.htm>

Great Buildings Online
<http://www.greatbuildings.com/>

Greek Art and Architecture
<http://harpy.uccs.edu/greek/index.html>

The Middle Ages
<http://www.learner.org/exhibits/middleages/>

Pyramids—The Inside Story
<http://www.pbs.org/wgbh/nova/pyramid/>

Renaissance: Symmetry, Shape, Size
<http://www.learner.org/exhibits/renaissance/symmetry_sub.html>

Roman Art and Architecture
<http://harpy.uccs.edu/roman/>

Roman Web
<http://www.hitchams.suffolk.sch.uk/roman/>

Skyscraper's Page
<http://www.iit.edu/~boonchu1/skyscraper.html>

Stenton Architecture
<http://www.stenton.org/history/>

Thais Greek Architecture
<http://www.thais.it/architettura/greca/indici/ind_micenea_uk.htm>

Featured Software Title

Fun with Architecture
<http://www.metmuseum.org/store/index.asp>
Created by the Metropolitan Museum of Art, Fun with Architecture allows students to utilize easy-to-use tools to create original architectural designs. Images can be easily exported for use in student publications and presentations. It is a must-have title for any elementary unit on architecture!

Building Understanding:

1. How can you tailor this unit to focus more closely on the building of relationships?

2. What local resources may contribute materials to your classroom for this unit?

3. Are there additional ways to bring in community involvement to your study of construction?

Assessment:

Figure 7.1—Construction Unit Participation Rubric

Participation	Needs Improvement 1	Satisfactory 2	Exemplary 3
Participates in class activities.	Occasionally when interested in the task.	Regularly whenever prompted to join.	Consistently with interest and enthusiasm.
Cooperates with peers.	Depends on whom he or she is working with.	Shares and works cooperatively.	Serves as a role model for sharing and cooperating.
Is a collaborative partner.	Does not share ideas or does not listen to others.	Collaborates to successfully complete tasks.	Is a class leader in forming collaborative partnerships.
Demonstrates an understanding of architectural design.	Does not demonstrate an understanding of architectural design.	Demonstrates a working understanding of architectural design.	Demonstrates a working understanding of architectural design which the learner then applies to new and different situations.
Demonstrated mastery of skills specified in state standards.	Did not meet the minimum requirements for state standards targeted in this unit.	Met the minimum requirements for state standards targeted in this unit.	Exceeded the minimum requirements for state standards targeted in this unit.

Figure 7.2—Construction Unit Project Rubric

Project	Needs Improvement 1	Satisfactory 2	Exemplary 3
Is done neatly with attention to detail.	Project is incomplete or lacks sufficient depth.	Project is neat and shows attention to detail.	Project is neat, shows attention to detail, and exhibits craftsmanship that goes beyond grade-level expectations
Is based in an identified content area of the unit.	Is not related to any content area being studied under the theme of construction.	Is based in one identified content area.	Is based in two or more identified content areas.
Applies skills and concepts in a new or different way.	Project imitates objects or examples studied in class.	Project demonstrates mastery of skills and concepts in a unique way.	Project demonstrates mastery of skills and concepts in a unique way at the highest level of thinking.
Adds to the class study of construction.	Does not add to the class experience or understanding of construction.	Adds to the class understanding of construction.	Adds to the class understanding of construction by elevating the level of discussion or activity.

Chapter $\boxed{8}$

Follow the Last Great Race on Earth

This Heroes unit sparks the imagination of students by inviting them to follow the Iditarod Sled Dog race online in real time. Each student or group of students selects a musher and dog team to follow and the result is lively, exciting learning about the hero that exists in each one of us!

AGE: Elementary School, but can be adapted to any grade level

Standards:

National English Language Arts Standards— *NCTE/IRA National Council of Teachers of English (2001).*

1. Apply a wide range of strategies to comprehend, interpret, evaluate, and appreciate texts. They draw on their prior experience, their interactions with other readers and writers, their knowledge of word meaning and of other texts, their word identification strategies, and their understanding of textual features (e.g., sound-letter correspondence, sentence structure, context, graphics).
2. Adjust use of spoken, written, and visual language (e.g., conventions, style, vocabulary) to communicate effectively with a variety of audiences and for different purposes.
3. Employ a wide range of strategies as they write and use different writing process elements appropriately to communicate with different audiences for a variety of purposes.
4. Use a variety of technological and information resources (e.g., libraries, databases, computer networks, video) to gather and synthesize information and to create and communicate knowledge.

5. Develop an understanding of and respect for diversity in language use, patterns, and dialects across cultures, ethnic groups, geographic regions, and social roles.

Standards for the English Language Arts, by the International Reading Association and the National Council of Teachers of English, Copyright 1996 by the International Reading Association and the National Council of Teachers of English. Reprinted with permission.

National Mathematics Standards—
NCTM National Council of Teachers of Mathematics (2000).

1. Understand meanings of operations and how they relate to one another.
2. Use mathematical models to represent and understand quantitative relationships.
3. Use visualization, spatial reasoning, and geometric modeling to solve problems.
4. Understand measurable attributes of objects and the units, systems, and processes of measurement.
5. Apply appropriate techniques, tools, and formulas to determine measurements.
6. Formulate questions that can be addressed with data and collect, organize, and display relevant data to answer them.
7. Develop and evaluate inferences and predictions that are based on data.
8. Understand and apply basic concepts of probability.
9. Solve problems that arise in mathematics and in other contexts.
10. Use the language of mathematics to express mathematical ideas precisely.

Standards are listed with the permission of the National Council of Teachers of Mathematics (NCTM). NCTM does not endorse the content or validity of these alignments.

National Science Standards—
NAS National Academy of Science (1995).

1. Changes in systems can be quantified. Evidence for interactions and subsequent change and the formulation of scientific explanations are often clarified through quantitative distinctions—measurement.

Reprinted with permission from "What Is the Influence of the National Science Education Standards?: Reviewing the Evidence, A Workshop Summary" (2003) by the National Academy of Sciences, courtesy of the National Academies Press, Washington, D.C.

National Social Studies Standards—
NCSS National Council for the Social Studies (1997).

1. The study of people, places, and human-environment interactions assists learners as they create their spatial views and geographic perspectives of the world.
2. People have wants that often exceed the limited resources available to them.
3. The realities of global interdependence require understanding the increasingly important and diverse global connections among world societies.

Permission to reprint standards granted by the National Council of Social Studies Publications.

THEME: *Heros*

! **Big Idea:** Heroes appear every day.

? **Need to Know Questions:**

1. Who can become a hero?
2. How does someone become a hero?
3. What are heroic actions?
4. Do events create heroes?
5. What traits do we admire in our heroes?

★ **Mission:** Read the following scenario to the class:

> "In the great white north, Inuit children are becoming gravely ill. From the symptoms that have been described, it seems that they are suffering from diphtheria. Doctors here in our community have the serum to help these children recover, but we need to be able to get the serum safely to those children who have no doctor or hospital nearby.
>
> The serum cannot be transported there by plane, train, truck, or car because of heavy snow and strong winds, and there are no places to stop for gas and supplies. Of course, the serum will have to be protected to get there safely, and it must arrive within two weeks of today. How can we save these children by getting the serum there safely and on time?"

Make a chart listing all the conditions under which the serum must be successfully delivered. Ask the class to make suggestions for transporting the serum that meet the conditions on the chart. Once everyone has exhausted suggestions, go through each solution and circle those ideas that meet all the conditions. Then have students vote on the solution they believe to be the best.

 Learning Tasks:

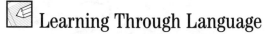 **Learning Through Language**

- Read children's literature about heroes, legends, and mythological characters.
- Study heroes in the traditional tales of other cultures.
- Research local heroes in your community.
- Write want ads for heroes to address problems in your community or state.
- Read biographies on mushers that participate in the Iditarod Sled Dog Race.
- E-mail mushers that your class will follow during the race.

- Make a dictionary of musher terms.
- Use and follow musher commands in the classroom.
- Send e-mail to other classes following the race.
- Keep a musher diary for the dog sled team your class follows in the race.

Learning Through Problem Solving

- Practice measuring distance on maps and across actual distances of your schoolyard.
- Study the time a musher takes to get from one checkpoint to the next on the trail and figure out his or her average speed on the trail.
- Construct a 9" x 12" map of the classroom or the school that uses a scale to accurately represent size.
- Devise a compass rose and legend for a classroom map or other maps.
- Sequence the checkpoints of the race in correct order from start to finish.
- Design a sled that is lighter and faster than the sleds currently used on the trail.
- Propose ways to measure how much work is being done when a dog team pulls a sled.
- Plan a strategy for winning the Iditarod that provides for good care of the dogs and efficient use of energy and time from the mountainous beginning of the trail to its flat, icy finish.
- Determine criteria for an optimal sled dog team and identify which teams have the best chance of winning the Iditarod.
- Explore how often a team's position at the start of the race (based on the bib number assigned to each musher) determines how well the team will finish the race.

Learning Through Seeing and Imagining

- Create a wall map of the Iditarod trail that shows major geographic features and each checkpoint along the trail.
- Have a team create sled dogs they can place on the wall map to mark the location of their mushers.
- Have each team follow the progress of its musher on the class wall map.
- Create a geographic mural that shows the major geographic features of Alaska.
- Examine digital pictures from the race online.
- Create a banner for your classroom celebrating the race.
- Make a digital collection of Inuit art.
- Study and create replicas of totem poles.
- Have students create an emblem to represent the dog sled team they are following in the race.
- Create a certificate of heroism using a desktop publishing program. Students can present the certificate to their dog sled team at the end of the race.

Learning Through Patterns

- Listen to songs about heroes and heroic acts.
- Find patterns common to mythology across cultures.
- Read poems of American heroes.
- Study Native American music.
- Study and create native American instruments.
- Listen to and make sounds of Alaskan nature.
- Cite patterns in features of different sled-racing dog breeds.
- Study different sled designs and find consistencies and differences.
- Identify patterns on the Iditarod trail.
- Listen to Web casts of the race.

 ## Learning Through Interaction with the Environment

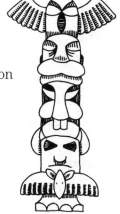

- Form a physical relief map of the Iditarod trail.
- Form students into simulated dog teams and take turns using musher commands to have the students move in proper direction as a team.
- Conduct different kinds of races and competitions between teams in your classroom.
- Make hero totems using available arts materials.
- Carve animals indigenous to Alaska out of soap.
- Build models of igloos using sugar cubes.
- Build original sled designs out of craft sticks.
- Create Iditarod Air Force planes using available classroom materials.
- Make homemade dog biscuits using a sugar cookie recipe.

- Test how fat creates insulation by filling a bucket of water and ice cubes, covering a student's hand in a sandwich bag, covering the outside of the sandwich bag with shortening and having the student immerse his or her covered hand in the ice water to see if he or she can feel the cold.

 ## Learning Through Interaction with Others

- Interview a community hero.
- Conduct a visit with a local dog trainer or kennel owner.
- Study the relationship between dogs and mushers.
- Explore the relationship between humans and the arctic environment.
- Identify an Alaskan food chain.
- Know the rules of safety and how they are enforced in the race.

- Work with a partner to improvise a scene on the trail.
- Form teams to follow mushers during the race.
- Take turns tracking your team's musher progress on the trail wall map.
- Collaborate online with other classes following the race.

♥ Learning Through Feelings, Values, and Attitudes

- Share personal heroes in our lives.
- Select a community hero to honor.
- List the characteristics common to all heroes.
- Identify current events that are in need of heroic action.
- Select a musher to follow during the race.
- Keep a musher journal of things learned during the race.
- Know the rules for participating in the Iditarod race.
- Study the role of the Iditarod Air Force in supporting the mushers and their dogs.
- Follow the care of the dogs during the race.
- Celebrate the tradition of the Red Lantern.

Learning Through Categories, Hierarchies, and Webbing

- Study the breeds of dogs used in the Iditarod.
- Survey and categorize Alaskan wildlife.
- Identify and sort Alaskan geographic features.
- Explore the weather and climate of Alaska.
- Identify different kinds of transportation useful in the Yukon.
- Research the midnight sun and the aurora borealis.
- Create a database of musher information.
- Sort the database by different queries.
- Compare the racing records of each musher.
- Rank the mushers according to class preference. Then rank them according to their finishes in last year's race. Note similarities and differences.

Learning Through Connections to Larger Understanding

- Study the history of the race.
- Inuit culture.
- Take a virtual tour of Mount McKinley and the Denali Mountains.
- Examine what is needed to survive in the arctic cold.
- Discuss the race as man against the elements.
- Research the impact diphtheria has on the body and on a community.
- Appreciate the role of women in the Iditarod.
- Understand the kinds of training necessary to be successful in the race.
- Identify the home states of mushers in the race.
- Create a Web site that celebrates your team's musher.

Culminating Event:

When the race begins in early March, have each team in your class follow the progress of its musher online and move its dog along the wall trail map you have created. Teams can also follow human interests through Alaskan news services and apply all they have learned as they cheer each sled dog team to Nome. Follow the race until its end when the Red Lantern is awarded—when the last team makes it safely to Nome.

 Resources:

 Books

Primary

    Adventures of Sparrowboy by Brian Pinkney

    Aunt Nancy and Old Man Trouble by Phyllis Root

    Dogs of the Iditarod by Jeff Schultz

    Drummer Hoff by Barbara and Ed Emberley

    Eggs Mark the Spot by Mary Jane Auch

    Johnny Appleseed by Steven Kellogg

    Livingstone Mouse by Pamela Duncan Edwards

    Loud Emily by Alexis O'Neill

    Mike Mulligan and His Steam Shovel by Virginia Lee Burton

    Ruby by Michael Emberley

    Where the Wild Things Are by Maurice Sendak

Elementary

    American Tall Tales by Mary Pope Osborne

    The Bunyans by Don and Audrey Wood

    D'Aulaires' Book of Greek Myths by Ingrid and Edgar Parin D'Aulaire

    Four of a Kind by Patti Sherlock

    John Henry by Ezra Jack Keats

    Little Ships: The Heroic Rescue at Dunkirk in World War II by Louise Borden

    Raisel's Riddle by Erica Silverman

    Red Flower Goes West by Ann Warren Turner

    Stone Fox by John Reynolds Gardiner

    Storm Run: The Story of the First Woman to Win the Iditarod Sled Dog Race by Libby Riddles

    Stuart Little by E.B. White

Middle School

    American Hero: The True Story of Charles A. Lindbergh by Barry Denenberg

    Black Star, Bright Dawn by Scott O'Dell

    Blackwater by Eve Bunting

    Call it Courage by Armstrong Sperry

    Confessions of a Teenage Drama Queen by Dyan Sheldon

    Dogsong by Gary Paulsen (see also *Dogteam* and *Woodsong*)

    Encounter by Jane Yolen

    Ishi, Last of His Tribe by Theodora Kroeber

Julie of the Wolves by Jean Craighead George
No Turning Back by Beverly Naidoo
Winterdance: The Fine Madness of Running the Iditarod by Gary Paulsen

High School

Call of the Wild by Jack London
Chocolate War by Robert Cormier
Don Quixote by Miguel de Cervantes
Great Expectations by Charles Dickens
The Iditarod Fact Book: A Complete Guide to the Last Great Race by Sue Mattson
Invisible Man by Ralph Ellison
Of Human Bondage by W. Somerset Maugham
Old Man and the Sea by Ernest Hemingway
A Portrait of the Artist as a Young Man by James Joyce
Seize the Day by Saul Bellow
Siddhartha by Herman Hesse

 Music

Carry on My Wayward Son—Kansas
Album: The Best of Kansas

The Greatest Love of All—Whitney Houston
Album: Whitney Houston

Hero—Mariah Carey
Album: Music Box

The Impossible Dream—various artists
Album: Man of LaMancha (Broadway soundtrack)

I've Got a Name—Jim Croce
Album: Photographs and Memories

Lean on Me—Bill Withers
Album: Lean on Me

Never Surrender—Corey Hart
Album: Boy in the Box

Running Down a Dream—Tom Petty
Album: Full Moon Fever

Where the Streets Have No Name—U2
Album: The Joshua Tree

Wind Beneath My Wings—Bette Midler
Album: Experience The Divine—Bette Midler Greatest Hits

@ Web Resources

Academy of Achievement
<http://www.achievement.org/autodoc/atv-index/>

Ageless Heroes
<http://www.pbs.org/kcet/agelessheroes/>

Anchorage Daily News
<http://www.adn.com/iditarod/>

Beyond Land's End
<http://beyond.landsend.com/iditarod/prologue>

Cabela's Iditarod Race Coverage
<http://www.cabelasiditarod.com/>

Discover Online
<http://www.discovery.com/area/exploration/iditarod/iditarod.html>

Dog sled.com
<http://www.dog sled.com/>

eIditarod Project
<http://surfaquarium.com/e_iditarod.htm>

Encyclopedia Mythica
<http://www.pantheon.org/mythica.html>

Greek Mythology
<http://www.mythweb.com/>

Happy Trails Kennel
<http://www.aviatornet.com/buserdog/>

Heroes for the Planet
<http://www.timeforkids.com/TFK/heroes/index.html>

Heroes of History
<http://www.heroesofhistory.com/>

Heroism in Action
<http://library.thinkquest.org/C001515/design/>

The Hero's Journey
<http://www.mcli.dist.maricopa.edu/smc/journey/>

Hometown Heroes
<http://www.weta.org/productions/hheroes/>

Iditarod Facts
<http://www.bena.com/lucidcafe/library/iditarod2.html>

Iditarod Ideas
<http://www2.grand-forks.k12.nd.us/ms/iditarod/iditarod.html>

My Hero
<http://www.myhero.com/New_features/home_11_04_01.asp>

Official Iditarod Site
<http://www.iditarod.com/>

Race Across Alaska
<http://teacher.scholastic.com/iditarod/home.htm>

Tilford on the Iditarod Trail
<http://www.vinton-shellsburg.k12.ia.us/tms/seventh/rdg7/iditarod/idit.html>

Time: Most Influential People of the 20th Century
<http://www.time.com/time/time100/time100poll.html>

Ultimate Iditarod
<http://www.ultimateiditarod.com/>

World Mythology
<http://www.windows.ucar.edu/cgi-bin/tour.cgi?link=/mythology/worldmap_new.html&sw=false&edu=mid&cd=false&v=&dr=&fr=f>

Featured Software Title

Neighborhood Map Machine
<http://www.tomsnyder.com/products/productdetail.asp?PS=NEIV20>
Tom Snyder Productions offers this elementary level application for creating maps from scratch, including images, sound, and video clips. Because it is fully customizable, Neighborhood Map Machine can be used over and over again in different areas of study, as students reinforce their map-making and map-reading skills.

Building Understanding:

1. What timeframe would you use for implementing this unit so that your class is ready to follow the Iditarod at the beginning of March?

2. What other kinds of heroism will you want to showcase in your unit study?

3. Is there a place for studying the anti-hero with your students? Could this encourage higher-level thinking where appropriate?

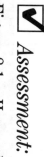

Assessment:

Figure 8.1—Heroes Unit Participation Rubric

Participation	Needs Improvement 1	Satisfactory 2	Exemplary 3
Participates in class activities.	Occasionally when interested in the task.	Regularly whenever prompted to join.	Consistently with interest and enthusiasm.
Cooperates with peers.	Depends on whom he or she is working with.	Shares and works cooperatively.	Serves as a role model for sharing and cooperating.
Is a collaborative partner.	Does not share ideas or does not listen to others.	Collaborates to successfully complete tasks.	Is a class leader in forming collaborative partnerships.
Demonstrates an understanding of heroism.	Does not demonstrate an understanding of heroism.	Demonstrates a working understanding of heroism.	Demonstrates a working understanding of heroism, which the learner then applies to new and different structures.
Demonstrated mastery of skills specified in state standards.	Did not meet the minimum requirements for state standards targeted in this unit.	Met the minimum requirements for state standards targeted in this unit.	Exceeded the minimum requirements for state standards targeted in this unit.

Figure 8.2—Heroes Unit Project Rubric

Project	Needs Improvement 1	Satisfactory 2	Exemplary 3
Is done neatly with attention to detail.	Project is incomplete or lacks sufficient depth.	Project is neat and shows attention to detail.	Project is neat, shows attention to detail, and exhibits craftsmanship that goes beyond grade-level expectations
Is based in an identified content area of the unit.	Is not related to any content area being studied under the theme of heroes.	Is based in one identified content area.	Is based in two or more identified content areas.
Applies skills and concepts in a new or different way.	Project imitates objects or examples studied in class.	Project demonstrates mastery of skills and concepts in a unique way.	Project demonstrates mastery of skills and concepts in a unique way at the highest level of thinking.
Adds to the class study of heros.	Does not add to the class experience or understanding of heros.	Adds to the class understanding of heros.	Adds to the class understanding of heros by elevating the level of discussion or activity.
Demonstrates high personal standards for work.	Does not demonstrate high personal standards in the completion of the project.	Demonstrates high standards for work as outlined by the teacher and/or class.	Demonstrates high personal standards for work that exceeds teacher expectations.

Chapter 9

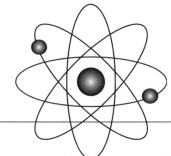

Exploring the

Future of Science

This Perspectives unit immerses students in the question of genetic engineering and its implications for society. What are the benefits of this ground-breaking new science? What are the dangers of allowing experimentation to occur without regulation? The culminating event is the sharing of position papers on the subject as the result of work in a Writer's Workshop program!

AGE: High School, but can be adapted to any grade level depending on the social topic you choose to examine with your students

Standards:

National English Language Arts Standards—
NCTE/IRA National Council of Teachers of English (2001).

1. Adjust use of spoken, written, and visual language (e.g., conventions, style, vocabulary) to communicate effectively with a variety of audiences and for different purposes.

2. Employ a wide range of strategies as they write and use different writing process elements appropriately to communicate with different audiences for a variety of purposes.

3. Apply knowledge of language structure, language conventions (e.g., spelling and punctuation), media techniques, figurative language, and genre to create, critique, and discuss print and non-print texts.

4. Students whose first language is not English make use of their first language to develop competency in the English language arts and to develop understanding of content across the curriculum.

5. Students participate as knowledgeable, reflective, creative, and critical members of a variety of literacy communities.

Standards for the English Language Arts, by the International Reading Association and the National Council of Teachers of English, Copyright 1996 by the International Reading Association and the National Council of Teachers of English. Reprinted with permission.

National Mathematics Standards—
NCTM National Council of Teachers of Mathematics (2000).

1. Formulate questions that can be addressed with data and collect, organize, and display relevant data to answer them.
2. Select and use various types of reasoning and methods of proof.
3. Recognize and apply mathematics in contexts outside of mathematics.

Standards are listed with the permission of the National Council of Teachers of Mathematics (NCTM). NCTM does not endorse the content or validity of these alignments.

National Science Standards—
NAS National Academy of Science (1995).

1. The present arises from materials and forms of the past. Interacting units of matter tend toward equilibrium states in which the energy is distributed as randomly and uniformly as possible.

Reprinted with permission from "What Is the Influence of the National Science Education Standards?: Reviewing the Evidence, A Workshop Summary" (2003) by the National Academy of Sciences, courtesy of the National Academies Press, Washington, D.C.

National Social Studies Standards—
NCSS National Council for the Social Studies (1997).

1. Personal identity is shaped by one's culture, by groups, and by institutional influences.
2. Institutions such as schools, churches, families, government agencies, and the courts all play an integral role in our lives.
3. Understanding the historical development of structures of power, authority, and governance and their evolving functions in contemporary U.S. society, as well as in other parts of the world, is essential for developing civic competence.
4. Technology forms the basis for some of our most difficult social choices.

Permission to reprint standards granted by the National Council of Social Studies Publications.

# THEME: *Perspectives*

! **Big Idea:** Everyone has a point of view to offer.

? **Need to Know Questions:**
1. How do you develop a voice of perspective?
2. In what ways can you share your perspective?
3. Can you consider more than one point of view?
4. Is one perspective as good as another?
5. How many perspectives should you consider in solving a problem?

★ **Mission:**

Read the following newsflash to the class:

"Scientists from a major university have announced that they have perfected a genetically engineered dog. This cloned canine barks 10 decibels quieter than any naturally occurring breed, does not shed, does not have bad breath, does not bite and comes completely house trained. This new dog design uses only one-third of the calories naturally existing breeds eat to live, and it does not seek to reproduce. You can add one of these genetically engineered specimens to your home by simply requesting the size and color you wish. Since they do not reproduce, you can order additional dogs as desired.

Lawmakers are scrambling to implement legislation on this astounding breakthrough in genetic engineering. They are looking for input from citizens on the value of allowing this kind of cloning to continue. Lawmakers are especially concerned with the question of whether this cloned dog should be allowed to be sold to families to keep in their homes. It raises many important questions about science and the ways in which it impacts our way of life."

Ask your students to consider this news and to share their reactions. Is this a great breakthrough in genetic engineering? Why or why not? Note important points made in the discussion on the board. Emphasize that all points of view will be heard and that all points of view will be respected. Conclude by asking students to continue to think about the ethics and implications of genetic engineering in our lives.

 Learning Tasks:

 Learning Through Language

- Read information books and periodicals on genetic engineering and cloning.
- Participate in a class debate on the pros and cons of genetic engineering in which there is no winner, but both sides are allowed to air the issues on the subject.

- Take a position on genetic engineering and discuss it as a class. Try to come to a consensus on the proper social policy and legislation for regulating cloning.
- Compare how different periodicals cover the topics of genetic engineering and cloning.
- Read editorials from online newspaper databases to get a sense for the different perspectives offered on genetic engineering and cloning.
- Study how propaganda is used in persuasive writing.
- Interview an expert on genetic engineering in person or online.
- Rewrite a traditional tale so that it includes cloning in the plot. Use the tale to help the reader consider the ramifications of genetic engineering on our existence.
- Generate a topic list on ethical scientific dilemmas for a Writing Workshop folder.
- Write a first draft based on one of the issues on your topic list.

Learning Through Problem Solving

- Map out the possible consequences for different kinds of genetic engineering.
- Compare the results you get from conducting the same search query on different search engines.
- Compare Web sites that present information on genetic engineering for format and content.
- Use information literacy strategies to determine which Web sites are the most reliable in their presentation of information.
- Generate and compare different proposals for legislating the regulation of genetic engineering.
- Rank proposals for regulating genetic engineering on specific criteria.
- Create a rubric that incorporates specific criteria in evaluating different proposals.
- Defer to the rules of correct grammar when writing.
- Practice well-developed paragraph construction by including a topic sentence and several supporting ideas.
- Edit a first (or subsequent) draft of an original piece of writing for technical errors.

Learning Through Seeing and Imagining

- Study an artist's perspective in paintings and photographs of animals.
- Examine satellite images of Earth from different points in the sky.
- Use an online map service to zoom in and out of a city map.
- View images under a microscope.
- Consider the different ways that Web sites are designed.
- Use a digital application to mirror, flip, and rotate 3-D images.
- Use QuickTime Virtual Reality to view 360-degree panoramic views of different locations online.

- Compare the characteristics of a cloned animal with those of a naturally reproduced animal of the same breed.
- Illustrate an opinion piece on genetic engineering once it is in final written form.
- Create a book layout for the story you are publishing.

❖ Learning Through Patterns

- Find patterns in public policy making that help us to predict the kinds of legislation that will be passed to regulate genetic engineering.
- Study the patterns of genetics found in heredity.
- Listen to songs that show different perspectives.
- Listen to different versions of the same song.
- Examine how background music can influence perspective.
- Create environmental sounds that influence perspective.
- Use musical instruments to create perspective.
- Compose a musical score that offers a unique perspective.
- Listen for perspective as someone reads his or her opinion piece orally.
- Identify patterns in your perspectives.

❀ Learning Through Interaction with the Environment

- Complete a task without using your sight.
- Complete a multi-person task without using language.
- Physically mirror, flip, and rotate a 3-D object.
- Rotate around an object to view it from different angles.
- View an object from different heights.
- Build models and create artwork that shows the view of an object from different perspectives.

- Participate in orienteering around your school grounds.
- Walk the school grounds and view the school from different streets or corners.
- Take a tour of your community and develop a perspective of each neighborhood.
- Bind your book once it is in publishable form.

🤝 Learning Through Interaction with Others

- Solicit literature from national organizations on both sides of the genetic engineering debate.
- Share your perspective on genetic engineering with classmates.
- Form debate teams based on opposing perspectives on genetic engineering.
- Survey your school on the issue of genetic engineering.
- Compare your perspective on genetic engineering with other classes and national polls and surveys.
- Visit with a local editor and discuss the importance of freedom of speech and freedom of the press when covering controversial topics.

- Conduct an online videoconference that brings together varied perspectives on genetic engineering.
- Conduct peer review writing sessions.
- Have regular writing conferences with students.
- Celebrate writing at a publishing party.

♥ Learning Through Feelings, Values, and Attitudes

- Determine your position on the ethics of genetic engineering.
- Express your opinion on genetic engineering by supporting it with facts.
- Write a letter to the editor of a local newspaper or Web site.
- Create a petition for your point of view on genetic engineering and gather signatures.
- Analyze survey data to find public support for your position on genetic engineering.
- Study the position of different political parties on genetic engineering.

- Conduct a class court case regarding the case of a cloned dog presented at the outset of this unit. Have students prepare a case for and against and serve as the judge for the trial.
- Write a well-developed first draft on genetic engineering.
- Conduct a self-assessment of your position piece.
- Revise a piece of writing based on feedback from peer review and writing conferences.

Learning Through Categories, Hierarchies, and Webbing

- Categorize arguments for and against genetic engineering and cloning.
- Examine the different points of view taken by Web sites on genetic engineering and cloning.
- Sort Web sites by points of view taken on genetic engineering and cloning.
- Examine the different perspectives on genetic engineering and cloning presented in newspapers.
- Create a semantic map of the different perspectives on genetic engineering and cloning.
- Categorize periodical articles on genetic engineering and cloning based on their perspectives.
- Create a classification system of the perspectives on cloning that includes a range of class perspectives on the subject.
- Use a checklist in your Writer's Workshop folder to keep track of each step of the writing process.
- Follow the prescribed steps in publishing your position piece on genetic engineering and cloning.

Learning Through Connections to Larger Understanding

- Study public opinion sampling.
- Prepare a critique of a work of art that includes a discussion of the artist's perspective.
- Write a literary criticism that includes the author's perspective on an ethical issue.
- Consider the impact of genetic engineering and cloning on society.
- Compare religious views on genetic engineering and cloning.
- Discuss ethical implications of genetic engineering.
- Compare different views of cloning in other cultures.
- Participate in a discussion board thread about genetic engineering and cloning.
- Create and use an online form to collect opinions on genetic engineering and cloning.
- Publish your opinion piece online.

▶ *Culminating Event:*

Celebrate student writing by having a publishing party at which works are shared and perspectives are discussed. Send the opinion pieces to your local newspaper for publication.

Resources:
Books

Primary

 Bad Case of Stripes by David Shannon
 Beware of Boys by Tony Blundell
 Bravest Ever Bear by Allan Ahlberg
 It's So Amazing: A Book About Eggs, Sperm, Birth, Babies and Families by
  Robie Harris
 Look Up, Look Down by Tana Hoban
 Seven Blind Mice by Ed Young
 Snail Spell by Joanne Ryder
 Sun and Moon: A Giant Love Story by Lisa Desimini
 That's Good, That's Bad by Margery Cuyler
 The True Story of the Three Little Pigs by A Wolf by John Scieszka
 Two Bad Ants by Chris Van Allsburg

Elementary

 Author: A True Story by Helen Lester
 Baa!: The Most Interesting Book You'll Ever Read About Genes and Cloning
  (Mysterious You) by Cynthia Pratt Nicolson, Rose Cowles
 Barefoot: Escape on the Underground Railroad by Pamela Duncan Edwards
 Korean Cinderella by Shirley Climo
 Jouanah by Tzexa Cherta Lee
 Mufaro's Beautiful Daughters by Jon Steptoe
 Stinky Cheese Man by Jon Scieszka
 Talking Eggs by Robert D. San Souci

Turkey Girl by Penny Pollack
What do Illustrators Do? by Eileen Christelow
Yeh Shen by Ai-Ling Louie

Middle School
Across the Lines by Carolyn Reeder
Anastasia Krupnik by Lois Lowry
Armageddon Summer by Jane Yolen
Bat 6 by Virginia Euwer Wolff
Cloning (Contemporary Issues Companion) by Lisa Yount
Crazy Lady! by Jane Leslie Conly
I Am an American: A True Story of Japanese Internment by Jerry Stanley
Journey by Patricia MacLachlan
Roll of Thunder, Hear My Cry by Mildred Taylor
Soldier Mom by Alice Mead
War with Grandpa by Robert Kimmel Smith

High School
The Bell Jar by Sylvia Plath
Catch-22 by Joseph Heller
The Chosen by Chaim Potok
The Debate over Human Cloning: A Pro/Con Issue (Hot Pro/Con Issue) by
    David Goodnough
Flowers for Algernon by Daniel Keyes
The Great Gatsby by F. Scott Fitzgerald
Heart of Darkness by Joseph Conrad
Monster by Walter Dean Myers
One Flew Over the Cuckoo's Nest by Ken Kesey
Pride and Prejudice by Jane Austen

 # Music

Both Sides Now—Judy Collins
Album: Colours of the Day

Daniel—Elton John
Album: Elton John—Greatest Hits 1970–2002

Hazy Shade of Winter—The Bangles
Album: Less Than Zero

Kodachrome—Paul Simon
Album: The Paul Simon Collection: On My Way, Don't Know Where I'm Goin'

Legend in Your Own Time—Carly Simon
Album: Anticipation

My Back Pages—The Byrds
Album: Byrds Play Dylan

My Old School—Steely Dan
Album: A Decade Of Steely Dan (Gold Disc)

Right Here, Right Now—Jesus Jones
Album: Doubt

Stand—R.E.M.
Album: Green

Teach Your Children—Crosby, Stills, Nash & Young
Album: So Far

 Web Resources

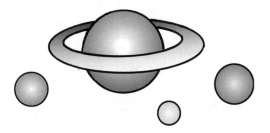

Aaron Shepard's Young Author's Page
<http://www.aaronshep.com/youngauthor/>

ABCs of the Writing Process
<http://www.angelfire.com/wi/writingprocess/>

Ace Writing
<http://www.geocities.com/fifth_grade_tpes/>

The Author Page
<http://www.ipl.org/div/kidspace/askauthor/>

The Big 6
<http://www.big6.com/showcategory.php?cid=6>

A Clone in Sheep's Clothing
<http://www.sciam.com/article.cfm?articleID=0009B07D-BD40-1C59-B882809EC588ED9F>

Cloning Fact Sheet
<http://www.ornl.gov/TechResources/Human_Genome/elsi/cloning.html>

Cracking the Code of Life
<http://www.pbs.org/wgbh/nova/genome/>

Designer Genes
<http://library.thinkquest.org/18258/>

Growth and Genetics
<http://www.brainpop.com/health/growthanddevelopment/>

Hidden New York
<http://www.pbs.org/wnet/newyork/hidden/index.html>

How Cloning Works
<http://www.howstuffworks.com/cloning.htm>

Incredible Story Studio
<http://www.storystudio.com/>

KidPub
<http://www.kidpub.org/kidpub/>

Mike Rofone: the Roving Reporter
<http://www.mikerofone.com/index.html>

New Scientist
<http://www.newscientist.com/hottopics/cloning/>

Ology
<http://www.ology.amnh.org/>

Page by Page: Creating a Children's Book
<http://www.nlc-bnc.ca/pagebypage/>

6 + 1 Trait Writing
<http://www.nwrel.org/assessment/department.asp?d=1>

Write Me a Story
<http://www.kidscom.com/create/write/write.html>

Writer's Workshop
<http://clerccenter.gallaudet.edu/Literacy/writerwk3.html>

The Write Site
<http://www.writesite.org/>

The Writing Process
<http://www.psesd.wednet.edu/write_process/write_PC/writepr.htm>

Writing Rubric Generator
<http://www.teach-nology.com/web_tools/rubrics/writing/>

Young Writers' Clubhouse
<http://www.realkids.com/club.shtml>

Featured Software Title

NetMeeting
<http://www.microsoft.com/windows/netmeeting/>
NetMeeting is bundled for free with Microsoft Windows, so you may very well
have it and not even realize it! All you need is an Internet connection and you
can perform live videoconferencing with other classes and experts from
around the world.

Building Understanding:

1. What resources do you have available to support online publishing of student work?

2. What do you need to do to have a Writing Workshop set up and in place when this unit begins?

3. Are there other local or national issues you would like to target in a Perspectives unit that tie in especially well to your curriculum?

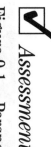

Assessment:

Figure 9.1—Perspectives Unit Participation Rubric

Participation	Needs Improvement 1	Satisfactory 2	Exemplary 3
Participates in class activities.	Occasionally when interested in the task.	Regularly whenever prompted to join.	Consistently with interest and enthusiasm.
Cooperates with peers.	Depends on whom he or she is working with.	Shares and works cooperatively.	Serves as a role model for sharing and cooperating.
Is a collaborative partner.	Does not share ideas or does not listen to others.	Collaborates to successfully complete tasks.	Is a class leader in forming collaborative partnerships.
Demonstrates an understanding of perspective.	Does not demonstrate an understanding of perspectives.	Demonstrates a working understanding of perspectives.	Demonstrates a working understanding of perspectives, which the learner then applies to new and different structures.
Demonstrated mastery of skills specified in state standards.	Did not meet the minimum requirements for state standards targeted in this unit.	Met the minimum requirements for state standards targeted in this unit.	Exceeded the minimum requirements for state standards targeted in this unit.

Figure 9.2—Perpectives Unit Project Rubric

Project	Needs Improvement 1	Satisfactory 2	Exemplary 3
Is done neatly with attention to detail.	Project is incomplete or lacks sufficient depth.	Project is neat and shows attention to detail.	Project is neat, shows attention to detail, and exhibits craftsmanship that goes beyond grade-level expectations
Is based in an identified content area of the unit.	Is not related to any content area being studied under the theme of perspectives.	Is based in one identified content area.	Is based in two or more identified content areas.
Applies skills and concepts in a new or different way.	Project imitates objects or examples studied in class.	Project demonstrates mastery of skills and concepts in a unique way.	Project demonstrates mastery of skills and concepts in a unique way at the highest level of thinking.
Adds to the class study of perspectives.	Does not add to the class experience or understanding of perspectives.	Adds to the class understanding of perspectives.	Adds to the class understanding of perspectives by elevating the level of discussion or activity.
Demonstrates high personal standards for work.	Does not demonstrate high personal standards in the completion of the project.	Demonstrates high standards for work as outlined by the teacher and/or class.	Demonstrates high personal standards for work that exceeds teacher expectations.

Chapter 10

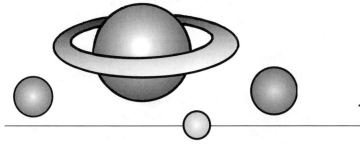

Building

an Interplanetary

United Nations

This Communication unit challenges students to consider the future of a world united with a common vision, and the role of that world in a larger community of life among the planets. The introduction of Lewis Carroll's *Jabberwocky* and the creation of original nonsense poems help to fuel discussion on communication as an essential part of the human condition. The culminating event is the formation of an Interplanetary United Nations in which each student participates as a delegate!

AGE: High School, but can be adapted to any grade level

Standards:

National English Language Arts Standards—
NCTE/IRA National Council of Teachers of English (2001).

1. Read a wide range of literature from many periods in many genres to build an understanding of the many dimensions (e.g., philosophical, ethical, aesthetic) of human experience.

2. Apply a wide range of strategies to comprehend, interpret, evaluate, and appreciate texts. They draw on their prior experience, their interactions with other readers and writers, their knowledge of word meaning and of other texts, their word identification strategies, and their understanding of textual features (e.g., sound-letter correspondence, sentence structure, context, graphics).

3. Employ a wide range of strategies as they write and use different writing process elements appropriately to communicate with different audiences for a variety of purposes.

4. Apply knowledge of language structure, language conventions (e.g., spelling and punctuation), media techniques, figurative language, and genre to create, critique, and discuss print and non-print texts.

5. Develop an understanding of and respect for diversity in language use, patterns, and dialects across cultures, ethnic groups, geographic regions, and social roles.

6. Use spoken, written, and visual language to accomplish purposes (e.g., for learning, enjoyment, persuasion, and the exchange of information).

Standards for the English Language Arts, by the International Reading Association and the National Council of Teachers of English, Copyright 1996 by the International Reading Association and the National Council of Teachers of English. Reprinted with permission.

National Mathematics Standards—
NCTM National Council of Teachers of Mathematics (2000).

1. Understand patterns, relations, and functions.
2. Recognize and apply mathematics in contexts outside of mathematics.

Standards are listed with the permission of the National Council of Teachers of Mathematics (NCTM). NCTM does not endorse the content or validity of these alignments.

National Science Standards—
NAS National Academy of Science (1995).

1. Types and levels of organization provide useful ways of thinking about the world.
2. Form and function are complementary aspects of objects, organisms, and systems in the natural and designed world.

Reprinted with permission from "What Is the Influence of the National Science Education Standards?: Reviewing the Evidence, A Workshop Summary" (2003) by the National Academy of Sciences, courtesy of the National Academies Press, Washington, D.C.

National Social Studies Standards—
NCSS National Council for the Social Studies (1997).

1. Human beings create, learn, and adapt culture.
2. Human beings seek to understand their historical roots and to locate themselves in time.
3. The study of people, places, and human-environment interactions assists learners as they create their spatial views and geographic perspectives of the world.
4. Understanding the historical development of structures of power, authority, and governance and their evolving functions in contemporary U.S. society, as well as in other parts of the world, is essential for developing civic competence.
5. The realities of global interdependence require understanding the increasingly important and diverse global connections among world societies.
6. An understanding of civic ideals and practices of citizenship is critical to full participation in society and is a central purpose of the social studies.

Permission to reprint standards granted by the National Council of Social Studies Publications.

THEME: *Communication*

 Big Idea: Communication builds understanding.

 Need to Know Questions:

1. What is effective communication?
2. What are the differences between verbal and nonverbal communication?
3. What are differences between online and face-to-face communication?
4. How can communication help solve problems?
5. How will communication change in the next 100 years?

⭐ **Mission:** Read the following scenario to the class:

Read the poem *Jabberwocky*, by Lewis Carroll, to the class. Work with your class to identify parts of speech in the poem based on the construction and context of nonsense words. Analyze the poem and come to a consensus on its meaning. Discuss how the poet was able to communicate to the reader without the use of conventional language.

🍎 *Learning Tasks:*

Learning Through Language

- Read stories that model different kinds of communication.
- Practice useful phrases from a foreign language.
- Create an original alphabet.
- Create nonsense parts of speech.
- Make a class book of nonsense words.
- View Web pages in different languages.
- Use an instant messenger application to play 20 questions.
- Conduct an online conversation.
- Write coded messages.
- Create original words to be used by inhabitants from a specific planet in our solar system.

Learning Through Problem Solving

- Derive rules of grammar from *Jabberwocky*.
- Decode messages that are received from classmates.
- Translate hieroglyphics online.

- Solve a problem with a partner without using oral or written language to communicate.
- Make acronyms.
- Study spoonerisms.
- Create palindromes.
- Construct anagrams.
- Complete a Lewis Carroll WebQuest.
- Devise strategies for how to communicate with citizens of other planets that help to break the language barrier between us.

Learning Through Seeing and Imagining

- Practice using a virtual search engine like Kartoo <http://www.kartoo.com/>.
- Use a visual thesaurus for reference <http://www.visualthesaurus.com>. Study similarities between alphabets.
- Examine how art communicates idea and emotion.
- Create "Who Am I?" slideshows in which each slide offers a clue and the last slide reveals the person, animal, or thing that is being described.
- Devise a visual form of communication that does not require speech in order to communicate.
- Catalogue different kinds of emoticons.
- Decode a rebus.
- Study international symbols.
- Create a set of interplanetary symbols.

Learning Through Patterns

- Manipulate sound waves at the Soundry <http://www.abc.lv/thinkquest/tq-entries/19537/main.html>.
- Study how sound communicates emotion.
- Communicate using sound, but not words or sentences.
- Practice using Morse code.
- Listen to songs from other cultures.
- Listen to songs about communication.
- Study the language patterns in *Jabberwocky*.
- Find patterns in nonsense poems.
- Write original nonsense poems.
- Study the patterns of organization in the United Nations.

Learning Through Interaction with the Environment

- Use sign language.
- Practice using nonverbal gestures in place of words.

- Act out an original silent movie scene.
- Act as a mime in specific situations.
- Take apart and rebuild an old telephone.
- Learn and practice flag signals.
- Have students pair up and take turns mirroring one another's body movements.
- Make human statues in which one student molds another student's body into a specific pose.
- Act out the action in *Jabberwocky* while the poem is read aloud.
- Reorganize your classroom to seat delegates from each planet of our solar system in an Interplanetary United Nations.

Learning Through Interaction with Others

- Discuss differences between the way humans and other living things communicate.
- Talk with senior citizens about how communication has changed in their lifetime.
- Listen to examples of entertainment and advertising from the Golden Age of radio.
- Create advertisements that would have communicated effectively to an audience 100 years ago.
- Run a class or school mail service.
- E-mail students who live in another part of the world.
- Participate in a mailing list discussion.
- Chat in an online community.
- Collaborate in groups on TappedIn <http://tappedin.org/>.
- Roleplay a model of a United Nation's general session in which each student represents a different country and the class discusses solutions to a common problem.

Learning Through Feelings, Values, and Attitudes

- Practice netiquette.
- Identify the values of American culture.
- Explore cultural mores from different parts of the world.
- Express your values on creating a world community in which all cultures are equal.
- Share common concerns about encountering intelligent life from other worlds.

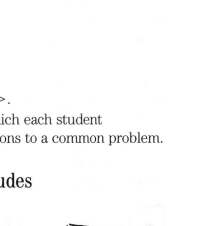

- Develop ideas on how citizens of Earth should interact with citizens of other planets.
- Write an interplanetary Bill of Rights.
- Negotiate rules for communication with other worlds.
- Survey people's attitudes on human interaction with life forms from other worlds.

Learning Through Categories, Hierarchies, and Webbing

- Analyze survey data in a spreadsheet format.
- Identify the attributes of parts of speech.
- Create nonsense words that match specific parts of speech.
- Categorize nonsense words by parts of speech.
- Build a database of nonsense words.
- Break down and analyze rhyme schemes in nonsense poetry.
- Web word maps that show relationships between nonsense words.
- Organize into planet-groups for a classroom United Nations simulation.
- Create an organizational map of an Interplanetary United Nations that includes all the planets of our solar system.

Learning Through Connections to Larger Understanding

- Explore the etymology of words.
- Conduct a cross-cultural online project.
- Take a virtual tour of another culture.
- Take a virtual tour of another planet.
- Imagine the source and meaning of radio waves from space.
- Have an alien visitor come to your classroom and attempt to communicate with your students.
- Study the potential for discovering other forms of intelligent life in outer space.
- Study the history of the United Nations.
- Plan an Interplanetary United Nations.
- Host an online presence of your class's Interplanetary United Nations.

▶ *Culminating Event:*

Set up your classroom as an Interplanetary United Nations-style forum and have each student serve as a representative from a different planet in our solar system. Have students share original nonsense poetry.

Or, set up a Web page that serves as an Interplanetary United Nations on which your student nonsense poems can be published.

◘ *Resources:*

 Books

Primary

> *Anansi and the Talking Melon* by Eric Kimmel
> *Bunny Cakes* by Rosemary Wells (see also *Max's First Word*)
> *Grandpa's Teeth* by Rod Clement

Hooway for Wodney Wat by Helen Lester
Martha Speaks by Susan Meddaugh
My Dog Is Lost! by Ezra Jack Keats
Quarreling Book by Charlotte Zolotow
Ruby Mae Has Something to Say by David Small
Somewhere Today: A Book of Peace by Shelley Moore Thomas
Very Quiet Cricket by Eric Carle
Whisper from the Woods by Victoria Wirth

Elementary
    Amber Brown Is Not a Crayon by Paula Danzinger
    Best Christmas Pageant Ever by Barbara Robinson
    Grandfather's Journey by Allen Say
    Home to Medicine Mountain by Chiori Santiago
    Knots on a Counting Rope by John Archambault
    Koko's Kitten by Francine Patterson
    La Mariposa by Francisco Jimenez
    Miss Rumphius by Barbara Cooney
    Rabbit Hill by Robert Lawson
    Stand up For Your Rights by Two-Can
    Wump World by Bill Peet

Middle School
    Among the Hidden by Margaret Peterson Haddix
    Basic Facts About the United Nations, 2000 by the United Nations
    Boat to Nowhere by Maureen Crane Wartski
    Illyrian Adventure by Lloyd Alexander
    Lily's Crossing by Patricia Reilly Giff
    Old Yeller by Fred Gipson
    Out of Darkness: The Story of Louis Braille by Russell Freedman
    Star Split by Kathryn Lasky
    Thank You, Jackie Robinson by Barbara Cohen
    Walker's Crossing by Phyllis Reynolds Naylor
    Weslandia by Paul Fleischman

High School
    *Act of Creation: The Founding of the United Nations: A Story of
        Superpowers, Secret Agents, Wartime Allies and Enemies, and Their
        Quest for a Peace* by Stephen Schlesinger
    The Color Purple by Alice Walker
    Cry, the Beloved Country by Alan Paton
    Death in Venice by Thomas Mann
    The Death of Artemio Cruz by Carlos Fuentes
    Farewell to Arms by Ernest Hemingway
    House of the Spirits by Isabel Allende
    The Learning Tree by Gordon Parks
    One Day in the Life of Ivan Denisovich by Aleksander Solzhenitsyn
    A Passage to India by E.M. Forster
    The Trial by Franz Kafka

Music

Burning Down the House—Talking Heads
Album: Sand in the Vaseline: Popular Favorites

Communication—Pete Townshend
Album: All The Best Cowboys Have Chinese Eyes

Does Anybody Really Know What Time It Is?—Chicago
Album: Chicago Transit Authority

Drive—The Cars
Album: Complete Greatest Hits

For What It's Worth—Buffalo Springfield
Album: Retrospective

Message in a Bottle—The Police
Album: Regatta de Blanc

Signs—The 5 Man Electrical Band
Album: Goodbyes and Butterflies

Talk to Me—Stevie Nicks
Album: Rock a Little

Walk Like an Egyptian—The Bangles
Album: Different Light

You've Got a Friend—James Taylor
Album: Greatest Hits

 # Web Resources

Acronym Finder
<http://www.acronymfinder.com/>

American Sing language Browser
<http://commtechlab.msu.edu/sites/aslweb/browser.htm>

American Sign Language Finger Spelling
<http://where.com/scott.net/asl/>

Anagram Genius Server
<http://www.anagramgenius.com/server.html>

Codes and Ciphers in the Second World War
<http://www.codesandciphers.org.uk/>

Decoding Nazi Secrets
<http://www.pbs.org/wgbh/nova/decoding/>

Emoticons
<http://www.computeruser.com/resources/dictionary/emoticons.html>

Improv Encyclopedia
<http://www.humanpingpongball.com/>

Jabberwocky Variations
<http://www76.pair.com/keithlim/jabberwocky/parodies/index.html>

Jim Kalb's Palindrome Connection
<http://www.palindromes.org/>

Kartoo
<http://www.kartoo.com/>

Kidz Page
<http://www.veeceet.com/>

Learn Improv
<http://www.learnimprov.com/>

Lewis Carroll Home Page
<http://www.lewiscarroll.org/carroll.html>

Listen and Write
<http://www.bbc.co.uk/education/listenandwrite/home.htm>

Morse Code Practice
<http://www.teklasoft.com/java/applets/morse/sfiles.htm>

Nonsense Poems
<http://f2.org/humour/language/nonsense.html>

Old Time Radio
<http://www.old-time.com/>

Quirkz Spoonerisms
<http://www.quirkz.com/verbal/spoon.html>

Rebus Rhymes
<http://www.enchantedlearning.com/Rhymes.html>

The Soundry
<http://www.abc.lv/thinkquest/tq-entries/19537/main.html>

TAPPS
<http://egghead.psu.edu/%7Ema_tapps/theatre/index.html>

The Ultimate Jabberwocky Page
<http://waxdog.com/jabberwocky/>

The United Nations
<http://www.un.org/>

United Nations Cyber School Bus
<http://www.un.org/Pubs/CyberSchoolBus/>

Featured Software Title

Dreamweaver
<http://www.microsoft.com/windows/netmeeting/>
Macromedia developed this popular WYSIWYG Web page editor that allows anyone the power
to create Web pages without having to know complicated HTML code. Intuitive and easy to
learn, Dreamweaver is a recommended component of a solid technology integration program.

✚ *Building Understanding:*

1. What is your personal communication style and how does it impact your delivery of instruction?

2. What local resources can you access to study how communication has changed in your community over the past century?

3. Is there an original theme you would like to develop into your own unit?

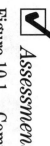

Assessment:

Figure 10.1—Communication Unit Participation Rubric

Participation	Needs Improvement 1	Satisfactory 2	Exemplary 3
Participates in class activities.	Occasionally when interested in the task.	Regularly whenever prompted to join.	Consistently with interest and enthusiasm.
Cooperates with peers.	Depends on whom he or she is working with.	Shares and works cooperatively.	Serves as a role model for sharing and cooperating.
Is a collaborative partner.	Does not share ideas or does not listen to others.	Collaborates to successfully complete tasks.	Is a class leader in forming collaborative partnerships.
Demonstrates an understanding of communication.	Does not demonstrate an understanding of communication.	Demonstrates a working understanding of communication.	Demonstrates a working understanding of communication, which the learner then applies to new and different structures.
Demonstrated mastery of skills specified in state standards.	Did not meet the minimum requirements for state standards targeted in this unit.	Met the minimum requirements for state standards targeted in this unit.	Exceeded the minimum requirements for state standards targeted in this unit.

Figure 10.2—Communication Unit Project Rubric

Project	Needs Improvement 1	Satisfactory 2	Exemplary 3
Is done neatly with attention to detail.	Project is incomplete or lacks sufficient depth.	Project is neat and shows attention to detail.	Project is neat, shows attention to detail, and exhibits craftsmanship that goes beyond grade-level expectations
Is based in an identified content area of the unit.	Is not related to any content area being studied under the theme of communication.	Is based in one identified content area.	Is based in two or more identified content areas.
Applies skills and concepts in a new or different way.	Project imitates objects or examples studied in class.	Project demonstrates mastery of skills and concepts in a unique way.	Project demonstrates mastery of skills and concepts in a unique way at the highest level of thinking.
Adds to the class study of communication.	Does not add to the class experience or understanding of communication.	Adds to the class understanding of communication.	Adds to the class understanding of communication by elevating the level of discussion or activity.
Demonstrates high personal standards for work.	Does not demonstrate high personal standards in the completion of the project.	Demonstrates high standards for work as outlined by the teacher and/or class.	Demonstrates high personal standards for work that exceeds teacher expectations.

Chapter 11

Assessment

Assessment Drives Instruction

When all is said and done, it is the assessment that drives instruction. From the beginning of the Building Bridges unit process, identifying the standards that will be covered throughout the course of study sets the tone for all other decisions made in the instructional design. Knowing your standards up front helps you keep in mind what you will assess, and knowing what you will assess drives the process of selecting theme, activities, and the paths to learning you will accommodate in your unit. As Wiggins and McTighe (38) say, teachers will do well to think less about instructional delivery and more about assessment in designing lessons and units. Good assessment drives good instruction.

The kinds of assessment you choose also impact the kinds of instruction you design. There's not much sense in offering all kinds of authentic learning tasks to your students and then settling students down for pencil and paper tests, any more than it makes sense teaching by lecture and class readings and then assessing student mastery by having them complete authentic tasks. Authentic learning requires authentic assessments. The follow through from assessment to instruction on this point is important: instructional tasks should match assessment tasks.

"What about state standardized tests? If I have my students performing authentic assessments, how will they ever be ready to fill in bubbles on an answer sheet?" Do you hear the fallacy in the assumption that is made in this statement? Forcing children to complete pencil and paper tasks all year will not make them any more prepared to successfully complete standardized tests according to their abilities. Rather, I would argue that children with a variety of authentic learning experiences and higher-level applications of the curriculum will fare *better* on standardized tests than students taught traditionally. Besides, the definition of mastery of a skill or concept is being able to successfully apply it in a new context. How well have our students mastered the state standards if they can only recognize them in a specific standardized format?

Good test takers don't know all the answers when they sit down on test day. Good test takers remain flexible and are able to apply what they have mastered in any situation to help them figure out the best answer to a question. Any standardized test can ask a student to label the parts of a closed circuit, but the student who is able to create a closed circuit from the necessary materials has truly mastered the concept. Which student would you rather have working for your business? This is the value of authentic assessment: to be able to demonstrate understanding in performance-based tasks. When students can show their learning in authentic ways, they not only have mastered the material, they have mastered the process of how to learn—a skill they will keep with them for a lifetime.

Does this mean we need to have an authentic assessment for every standard that we identify at the outset of a unit? Thankfully, no. Plan your assessments so that by the time your students contribute to the unit's culminating event, they can show their mastery of the standards through their authentic work products. In this way, students will have the chance to demonstrate their mastery regardless of their strengths and they will have the opportunity to strengthen other paths to learning, which they may need more experience in developing.

Rubric Construction

If assessment is the key, then the way in which you assess authentic tasks is extremely important. I encourage you to devise open-ended tasks that allow each student to apply the skills and concepts you have taught in novel ways. This is where the LoTi level of Expansion and Refinement truly comes in to play for technology integration. Give students the room to select their own approach to addressing the issue you have presented at the outset of the unit, allow them access to all kinds of technology, facilitate student work and collaboration as work products begin to take shape, and provide the structure needed to bring together all of your class' work into one culminating event that celebrates achievement. The possibilities are all around you. It simply requires each of us to look at assessment with a different point of reference, rather than addressing each standard individually in isolation.

The authentic assessment tool of choice is the rubric. Rubrics offer both quantitative evaluation of student work while offering qualitative feedback. If the teacher has the criteria for student work in place at the outset of the unit, students can use the rubric as their guide for successfully participating in the work before them. It's a win-win situation.

When constructing rubrics:

- Share the rubric with students and discuss it for clarification; allow for the possibility that students may have suggestions that you will want to add to the rubric as the unit gets underway
- Create the rubric in a spreadsheet so that it is easy to fill in, calculate, and save (this saves on paper too).

- Use indicators for degrees of success that are highly descriptive and include numerical weights; in this way, students can see differentiated levels of success and grading becomes much easier to accomplish.
- Have students complete the rubric on their own work in progress, then share their perceptions with you before you complete the rubric on their product.

For example, consider the rubrics from the Frontiers unit in Chapter 4, one for participation and one for their work product:

Using these rubrics, the student scores out of a possible 15 points on each. You will want to determine what the minimum score is to pass each part of the assessment. Is there any doubt that after completing this assessment both the student and teacher will know to what degree the student has mastered the standards for the unit? Is there any question that students who perform at the Excellent level of the rubric will do well on any standardized test with regard to these standards? A well-constructed rubric is a strong teaching and assessment tool.

Building Understanding:

1. Are you comfortable choosing your assessment strategy before you develop your unit of instruction? Why or why not?

2. How can you create an assessment tool that measures student mastery of stated standards without creating an individual rubric for each standard?

3. What other forms of authentic assessment would you be interested in using in addition to rubrics? Which tool are you most comfortable in using for authentic assessment? Why?

Assessment:

Figure 11.1—Frontiers Unit Participation Rubric

Participation	Needs Improvement 1	Satisfactory 2	Exemplary 3
Participates in class activities.	Occasionally when interested in the task.	Regularly whenever prompted to join.	Consistently with interest and enthusiasm.
Cooperates with peers.	Depends on whom he or she is working with.	Shares and works cooperatively.	Serves as a role model for sharing and cooperating.
Is a collaborative partner.	Does not share ideas or does not listen to others.	Collaborates to successfully complete tasks.	Is a class leader in forming collaborative partnerships.
Demonstrates characteristics of an explorer.	Does not like to take risks or explore unknown subject matter.	Takes risks and seeks support to explore the unknown.	Takes risks, seeks support, and uses critical-thinking skills to explore the unknown.
Demonstrated mastery of skills specified in state standards.	Did not meet the minimum requirements for state standards targeted in this unit.	Met the minimum requirements for state standards targeted in this unit.	Exceeded the minimum requirements for state standards targeted in this unit.

Figure 11.2—Frontiers Unit Project Rubric

Project	Needs Improvement 1	Satisfactory 2	Exemplary 3
Is done neatly with attention to detail.	Project is incomplete or lacks sufficient depth.	Project is neat and shows attention to detail.	Project is neat, shows attention to detail, and exhibits craftsmanship that goes beyond grade-level expectations
Is based in an identified content area of the unit.	Is not related to any content area being studied under the theme of frontiers.	Is based in one identified content area.	Is based in two or more identified content areas.
Applies skills and concepts in a new or different way.	Project imitates objects or examples studied in class.	Project demonstrates mastery of skills and concepts in a unique way.	Project demonstrates mastery of skills and concepts in a unique way at the highest level of thinking.
Adds to the class study of frontiers.	Does not add to the class experience or understanding of frontiers.	Adds to the class understanding of frontiers or explorers.	Adds to the class understanding of frontiers or explorers by elevating the level of discussion or activity.
Demonstrated high personal standards for work.	Does not demonstrate high personal standards in the completion of the project.	Demonstrates high standards for work as outlined by the teacher and/or class.	Demonstrates high personal standards for work that exceeds teacher expectations.

Works Consulted

Armstrong, T. *Multiple Intelligences in the Classroom*. Alexandria, VA: Association for Supervision and Curriculum Development, 2000.

Bruner, J.S. *Toward a Theory of Instruction*. Cambridge, MA: Belknap, 1966.

Bruner, J.S. *Actual Minds, Possible Worlds*. Cambridge, MA: Harvard University Press, 1986.

Bruner, J.S. & Bornstein, M.H. *Interaction in Human Development*. Hillsdale, NJ: Erlbaum, 1989.

Bruner, J.S., Goodnow, J. & Austin, G.A. *A Study of Thinking*. New York: Wiley, 1956.

Bruner, J.S., Oliver, R. & Greenfield, P.M. *Studies in Cognitive Growth*. New York: Wiley, 1966.

Fogarty, R. *The Mindful School How to Integrate the Curricula*. Arlington Heights, Illinois: IRI Skylight, 1999.

Gardner, H. *Frames of Mind: The Theory of Multiple Intelligences*. New York: Basic Books, 1983.

Jacobs, H.H. *Interdisciplinary Curriculum: Design and Implementation*. Alexandria, VA: Association for Supervision and Curriculum Development, 1989.

Jacobs, H.H. *Mapping the Big Picture: Integrating Curriculum & Assessment K–12*. Alexandria, VA: Association for Supervision and Curriculum Development, 1997.

McKenzie, W. *Multiple Intelligences and Instructional Technology: A Manual for Every Mind*. Eugene, OR: International Society for technology in Education, 2002.

Moersch, C. Levels of technology implementation (LoTi): A framework for measuring classroom technology use. *Learning and Leading with Technology*, 1995: 40–42.

National English Language Arts Standards. 2001. Retrieved September 7, 2003, from the National Council of Teachers of English Web site <http://www.ncte.org/standards/standards.shtml>.

National Science Education Standards. 1995. Retrieved September 7, 2003, from the National Academy of Science Web site <http://www.nap.edu/readingroom/books/nses/>.

National Standards for Social Studies Teachers. 1997. Retrieved September 7, 2003, from the National Council for the Social Studies Web site <http://www.socialstudies.org/standards/teachers/vol1/home.shtml>.

Piaget, J. *Science of Education and the Psychology of the Child*. New York: Viking, 1969.

Principles and Standards for School Mathematics. 2000. Retrieved September 7, 2003 from the National Council of Teachers of Mathematics Web site <http://standards.nctm.org/document/index.htm>.

Sternberg, R.J. (Ed.). *Mechanisms of Cognitive Development*. New York: Freeman, 1984.

Sternberg, R.J. *Beyond IQ: A triarchic Theory of Human Intelligence*. New York: Cambridge University Press, 1985.

Taylor, R.T. *Connecting the Curriculum Using an Integrated, Interdisciplinary, Thematic Approach*. Alexandria, VA: Association for Supervision and Curriculum Development, 1993.

Wiggins, G. & McTighe, J. *Understanding by Design*. Alexandria, VA: Association for Supervision and Curriculum Development, 1998.

Vygotsky, L.S. *Mind in Society*. Cambridge, MA: Harvard University Press, 1978.

Vygotsky, L.S. *Thought and Language*. Cambridge, MA: M.I.T. Press, 1962.

Index